THE FACILITATION
ADVANTAGE

Build Relationships, Drive Impact, Lead with Influence

Kat Koppett and Therese Miclot

The Facilitation Advantage:
Build Relationships, Drive Impact, Lead with Influence

Kat Koppett and Therese Miclot

For information, contact
BDI Publishers, Atlanta, Georgia
bdipublishers@gmail.com

Kat Koppett kat@koppett.com and
Therese Miclot therese.miclot@me.com

Cover Design and Layout: Tudor Maier
BDI Publishers

Atlanta, Georgia

ISBN: 978-0-9862965-3-6

In loving memory of our fathers, Leonard Koppett and Norman N. Mlachak, esteemed journalists whose ink and passion for storytelling shaped our own literary paths.

This book is a tribute to their legacy, a testament to their enduring influence, and a heartfelt expression of gratitude for the gift of words they imparted to us.

CONTENTS

Introduction

I t's 7:55 a.m. and attendees are arriving slowly. As we greet everyone, we can almost read their minds, and it's not encouraging. Some are thinking *Not another meeting*, others are wondering *Will this really go until 4 o'clock?* As they type last-minute emails, several attendees telegraph mild panic on their faces — *I've got a hundred other important things I need to do* — while a couple are just here for the pastries.

A few are even thinking, *I care about this topic, and I'm worried it won't be presented in the right way, so we will miss our chance to make a real impact.*

We get it.

One person drones on, topics go off track, and the elephant in the room — the purpose of the session — remains unacknowledged. Hours get wasted, and results remain unrealized. Whether it is a sales pitch, a weekly team meeting, or a presentation, the bar is incredibly low for most facilitated events. But it does not have to be that way.

Although we - Kat and Therese - come from different backgrounds, we bonded over our shared belief in the power of core leadership skills for effective facilitation; skills that evolved over time and will be featured in this book. Kat's path began as a professional actor and improviser, and eventually led to getting a degree in organizational psychology. She used her combined experience to mash up improvisational theater, storytelling, and experiential learning and organizational development theory to help develop the field of applied improvisation.

Therese started her career in human resources after earning a master's degree in industrial/organizational psychology. Her focus area was ensuring leaders were ready and equipped to execute a company's business strategy. She traveled around the world to deliver leadership skills training, then began coaching and developing others' facilitation skills.

When we met while working for a large social media company that threw us together on manager development and facilitation excellence projects, it became clear that the sum of our work transcended our individual practices. Our collaboration — and the framework you will explore in this book — was born.

We have coached and developed thousands of leaders from around the globe, from managers to senior executives. One of the most important skills effective leaders possess, no matter their role, is the ability to not only communicate but catalyze others to act. This is not just a business or workplace issue. In an increasingly fractured world facing immediate and dire challenges to our very existence, we all need facilitation skills.

This book puts the essential ingredients for transforming not-so-great interactions into productive, engaging, and inclusive ones in your hands. Consider it your how-to guide for facilitating any interaction at any time or place, either virtually or in person. Whether you are looking for a quick tip to address a challenge in the moment or a comprehensive road map for developing facilitation skills in the long term, we invite you to explore these practical approaches.

1. Facilitation Skills
Are Leadership Skills

What is facilitation? Surprisingly, the International Association of Facilitators (IAF), the most respected association for professionals in the field, does not have an official single definition for a facilitator. That is sort of amazing, right? And it delights us.[1]

The word *facilitate* comes from the Latin root, *facilis*, which means to "make easy, render less difficult." We crave leaders who can make it easier to work cohesively, clear the way for diverse perspectives that drive innovative solutions, and remove obstacles to achieve results.

At the core of leadership lies facilitation that looks like this:

 A subject matter expert tailors their message, making it easier for their audience to understand the subject at hand.

 A project manager transforms meetings from mundane to meaningful.

 A solutions architect guides a team through an unexpected challenge.

 A senior leader creates the conditions for people to be candid and vulnerable and feel included.

 A nonprofit leader engages volunteers and donors in a meaningful way.

1 International Association of Facilitators does not have a single, official definition.

Facilitation skills serve as a force multiplier for leader effectiveness. They enable leaders to foster open and honest communication and thereby encourage the exchange of ideas and feedback crucial for informed decision-making. Leaders with strong facilitation skills resolve conflicts swiftly and maintain team cohesion and productivity. These skills also help leaders nurture a culture of collaboration, innovation, and inclusivity, which enhances team morale and performance. Ultimately, facilitation skills amplify a leader's impact, enabling them to navigate complex challenges, inspire their teams, and achieve exceptional results.

Facilitation skills do not belong just to some rarefied breed of credentialed professionals. Admittedly, just as there are Michelin-star chefs who engage with food using skills and talents that go beyond what most of us — even those of us who love to cook — will ever aspire to, there are elite professional facilitators. The field of facilitation, however, like cooking, offers an opportunity for lifelong learning. As in cooking, you don't have to be a top-level facilitator to glean the satisfaction and impact of a little bit of knowledge and practice in the arena. Just as any kid who has scrambled messy eggs, stuck a couple of pieces of bread in a toaster, or presented a perfect breakfast in bed for Mother's Day, can attest a little facilitation skill can go a long way.

Oh, what a difference these often-unnoticed but powerful facilitation contributions can make to both the experience and results of our interactions!

But what is it that separates leaders who are effective facilitators from their not-so-effective counterparts? This is the key question we set out to answer: What are the core knowledge, skills, and mindsets that are most easily available to the home chef — uh, facilitator?

At its essence, facilitation involves making choices, moment to moment, that support others and identified desired outcomes. When working with others, you have options: Present data, share an anecdote, ask a question, teach, demonstrate, initiate a conversation, listen, and hold silence. You can take up lots of space or very little. You can stick to a preplanned agenda with strict discipline or create a flow in the moment. What separates good cooks from mediocre ones, we believe, separates effective facilitators, and comes down to three traits:

1. **Awareness** of the ingredients at your disposal.
2. The **choices** you make about which ingredients to use.
3. Your **skill** in using those ingredients.

We will support you in each of these steps.

In terms of identifying ingredients, long lists of individual spices, vegetables, proteins, and so on (for our purposes here: tips, tricks, and tools) can become overwhelming and unhelpful in the moment. But many facilitation training books and programs seem to offer just that.

Throughout our years of facilitating and of coaching and training other leaders to facilitate, we have organized these tips, tricks, and tools approaches, beliefs, processes, and mindsets into one framework that will help you understand what is in your facilitation "pantry." Organizing the ingredients into categories makes it easier to make choices as you build and employ your facilitation skills.

We call these categories of facilitation skills contributions.

Note that this is *not* a recipe book. There are too many different contexts, styles, and personal tastes for paint-by-the-numbers approaches like that to be useful. Rather, we offer a way to understand when and how you might decide to employ one skill rather than another — why, for example, you might give a 10-minute talk versus ask a question or tell a story.

Bottom line: There is almost never one right answer to what facilitation move to make; there are almost always great questions to have ready to ask yourself.

Leaders do not improve just with knowledge. As much as we obsessively watch *The Great British Bake Off*, neither of us can whip together a sculpted bread lion complete with almond claws, or even a simple rose, lychee, and raspberry fruit tart. Skills take practice, so our framework includes behaviors — ways to identify what the ingredients look and sound (taste?) like, so you can grow them yourself.

With your indulgence, we will extend the cooking metaphor for one more moment.

Like cooking, facilitation is an art. We believe strongly in the value of science — and as learning and development practitioners, we attempt to ground our methods in evidence-based practices as much as possible — but we are practitioners, not researchers. We do not mean to imply that these contributions are some objectively tested model, like the periodic table of elements, that will interact in a reliable, predictable way when added together in certain percentages. And we do not profess to offer some objective, sole definition of facilitation. The intentions of this framework are to inspire and guide you in the development of useful skills.

Disclaimer firmly in place, here are the ways to amplify your leadership.

Our model of ten facilitation contributions is divided into three groups: mindset, content, and process. We call them contributions because they are the "gifts," or offerings, facilitators bring to a group. The framework is *not* a cycle to be followed in order. The contributions intersect with and support each other — the sum is greater than the parts — and although we have divided the ten into these three groups, there are mindset, content, and process components in each contribution.

We discuss each contribution in the chapters that follow. Here is a short introduction to each.

Mindset

Everyone carries their own set of values, preferences, habits, triggers, biases, and insecurities. The contributions **Manage Yourself** and **Model Values and Beliefs** address the internal and external work that facilitators must do to expand their conscious awareness of these attributes; demonstrate positive behaviors in alignment with their professed beliefs; and manage their biases, unhelpful habits, and impulses. It is only on this strong foundation that a facilitator can dependably show up at their best, set a productive environment, and serve the needs of the group.

Manage Yourself

Before we can engage effectively with others, we must be able to handle ourselves effectively. Managing yourself involves managing your body, recognizing your triggers and biases, and monitoring your self-talk so you can stay focused on your goal.

Model Values and Beliefs

Both in and outside formal environments, leaders hold privileged positions, handling high-stakes conversations and guiding groups. To be effective and get the results we want, we must demonstrate the core values we profess to believe in. Learn how to align with your values, enabling you to show up authentically, create a productive environment, and serve the needs of the group.

Content

Share Subject Matter and **Suit the Context** competencies are inextricably linked. The same information may prove helpful and relevant in one context and wildly inappropriate and useless in another.

Share Subject Matter

When people look to us as a credible source of information and expertise, we provide relevant knowledge and skills that inform the interaction. Even when it's not required to be the subject-matter expert, having knowledge and skills in a subject allows you to uncover the root of issues, offer solutions, and build capability in others.

People don't expect facilitators to have all the answers all the time, but they do expect the content to be offered in their unique context.

Suit the Context

Every group operates in an environment that's uniquely theirs — the people, the challenge, the culture. It's the facilitator's job to understand content in relation to context and create a tailored experience.

A skilled facilitator recognizes that the same event with a different person, team, or organization is a different experience. Understanding context allows us to tailor our approach and offer the right content in a way that produces results.

Process

Most interactions succeed or fail based on the quality of the process. We watch how people **Establish Presence** with their bodies, voices, and words. We're wired to pay attention to those verbal and nonverbal signals. When we **Engage with Story**, the content becomes more effective and memorable. Great facilitative leaders **Listen** deeply first and ensure they understand other points of view before advocating for their own opinions. Then they build on what people say by adapting for impact and keeping on track by **Serving the Purpose.**

Contributions are often felt when they are absent. Meetings frequently suffer when the leader fails to **Balance Risk and Safety** by not calibrating to how much challenge or comfort people need. A great facilitator goes beyond just providing information. They add value and **Support Development** through feedback and guidance that help people grow.

Establish Presence

We trust and follow those who project confidence and credibility. We observe people with presence and notice how they use their body, voice, and words. Effective facilitators speak and move with authority, hold space for others, and give and take focus intentionally. Even their silence has the power to influence and create connection.

Engage with Story

Story is the oldest and most robust of communication and learning tools. Almost everyone responds deeply to stories because we've been using them to share important ideas and information since the dawn of humanity.

Using storytelling skills deliberately enlivens a presentation, deepens understanding, increases retention, and builds credibility.

Listen

We crave leaders who listen. It's the foundation for all human connection. It requires us to shelve our own agendas temporarily, activate our curiosity, and take in all that's being said and not said. In return, we gain a greater breadth and depth of relevant information and insights. When people feel seen, heard, and understood, they are more likely to engage.

Serve the Purpose

The clock on the wall says you are 15 minutes behind on the agenda, but the conversation is lively and engaged. Do you stick to the plan or improvise? At the very heart of good facilitation lies our ability to make these calls effectively. Beyond mere time management, Serve the Purpose is about knowing your goals and expanding your options to reach them best.

Balance Risk and Safety

Balancing risk and safety involves offering the right level of support and challenge to people. This requires specific attention to the needs of the individual and group. Without a little push — without being presented with a challenge, we can remain stuck in our comfort zones, and opportunities can be missed. Hitting the sweet spot increases engagement and results.

Support Development

The value we offer to others goes beyond simply leading meetings or giving presentations well. In every interaction, we also have the opportunity to support the development of others. Learn how to give feedback and coach in a way that enables people's growth.

The Contributions in Practice

In virtually all walks of life, when leaders understand the contributions, they can make choices intentionally that lead to better outcomes. Remember the foundational premise of this book:

Anyone who leads should be able to facilitate well.

Imagine a day in the life of a sales leader. Some meetings require more talking, while other times, a sales leader needs to listen more to address a problem or resolve a conflict. During a high-stakes sales meeting, the leader might need to manage their own mindset when a curveball question comes their way or tell a compelling story when noticing a confused look on a client's face.

This chart shows the steps in the process through the lens of "a day in the life."

Day in the Life of a Sales Leader

	7:30 am	10:00 am	Noon	2:00 pm	5:00 pm
	Meeting with direct report	Prep for a client meeting with product team	Present new sales targets to team	Lead client presentation	Update leaders on quarterly sales results
Manage Yourself				✔	✔
Model Values	✔		✔	✔	
Share Subject Matter/Suit Context		✔	✔	✔	✔
Engage with Story		✔	✔	✔	
Establish Presence		✔	✔	✔	✔
Listen	✔	✔		✔	✔
Serve the Purpose			✔	✔	
Balance Risk and Safety				✔	
Support Development	✔		✔		

A project leader might lead a weekly team meeting, but mostly listen to others give their reports. When the meeting gets side-tracked, they know how to bring everyone's attention back to the priorities.

During their weekly one-on-one with their manager, they pitch an idea for a new project and get approval. Woot! Throughout the afternoon and evening, their various meetings require additional combinations of contributions based on the varying goals and contexts.

Day in the Life of a Project Leader

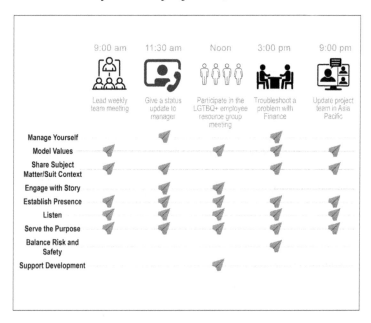

Your Turn

Before reading further, it will be helpful to get a sense of your current relationship to these contributions. How familiar are you with each? How well do you demonstrate them now?

Use this short self-assessment to think about how you show up to others in a specific context that is most relevant to you. Objectively rate how well you consistently do these tasks, then average your score for each contribution.

If you're not ready for the self-assessment now, consider returning to it after diving further into the book.

The Facilitation Advantage Self-Assessment			
Rate yourself on how you operate when working with groups.	**1** I Need to Learn It	**2** I Need to Do More of It	**3** I Do It Consistently
Manage Yourself Nurtures overall well-being and healthy mindsets	Self-Rating		Average *(add your self-ratings and divide by 4)*
I maintain my energy and health.			
I am aware of my personal triggers and have strategies to manage them.			
I am conscious of bias and have tools to minimize it.			
I recognize and address my unsupportive self-talk.			
Model Values and Beliefs Aligns actions and words with principles	Self-Rating		Average
I have identified my core values and beliefs.			
My behaviors align with my values and beliefs.			
I work to understand others' values and beliefs.			
I take others' beliefs and values into account when interacting.			
Share Subject Matter Displays expert knowledge and relates content to audience priorities	Self-Rating		Average
I possess relevant principles and knowledge.			
I model relevant skills and abilities.			
I scale my expertise to the needs and experience of others.			
I hold my expertise with humility and am open to correction and new insights.			

Suit the Context Demonstrates an understanding of group history, norms, and culture	Self-Rating	Average
I gather relevant information about the history, experiences, and values of those I will engage with.		
When interacting, I can speak about the group's dynamics, history, and culture accurately.		
I notice and understand specific group dynamics.		
I honor others' experience and needs by tailoring how I relate my expertise.		

Establish Presence Confidently holds the space with credibility, patience, humility, and authenticity	Self-Rating	Average
I can use my body, voice, and words intentionally to give and take focus.		
I understand the language of status and power dynamics.		
I recognize my habitual behaviors and power comfort zone.		
I can adapt my behavior to claim or offer attention and respect.		

Engage with Story Enlivens interactions and deepens understanding with anecdotes and strong narratives	Self-Rating	Average
I enrich my communication with anecdotes, examples, and personal experiences.		
I use narrative structures to aid understanding and recall.		
I discern and address ambient narratives.		
I elicit stories from others to enhance insight, connection, and commitment.		

Listen Seeks to connect deeply with others, hearing both the spoken and unspoken, and supporting them where they are	Self-Rating	Average
I demonstrate active listening by paying attention not just to words, but also to intentions, values, and emotions.		
I proactively seek out and acknowledge all points of view, even when they differ from my own.		
I actively summarize and integrate the reactions and insights of others.		
I spark meaningful interactions by asking thought-provoking questions that encourage genuine participation and foster deeper engagement.		

Serve the Purpose Balances keeping on track and adapting for impact	Self-Rating	Average
I clarify the purpose and goals to provide focus and direction.		
When the group goes off track, I redirect them to bring the focus back to the purpose and goal.		
I make adjustments when the process is no longer serving the group or the desired outcome.		
I manage unexpected challenges and events with grace and calm.		

Balance Risk and Safety Provides the right level of support and challenge to the individual and group	Self-Rating	Average
I assess what's needed to increase feelings of safety or reduce perceived risks.		
I create opportunities to stretch and explore new possibilities without fear of shame or punishment.		
I ensure everyone feels safe in expressing their perspectives.		
I model and acknowledge vulnerability.		

Support Development Provides insights and opportunities for individual and group growth	Self-Rating	Average
I create the conditions that encourage people to accept my support.		
I guide people in reflecting on their own behaviors.		
I offer specific, timely feedback that includes the impact of a decision or action.		
I help individuals and teams reach their potential.		

Now that you have a snapshot of your current facilitation capability, you have some context for how to best engage with this book. There are many right ways.

If your total average is in the "I Need to Learn It" category (< 2), no worries! You've come to the right place. You can dive in and read this book from cover to cover, extracting all the compelling and practical wisdom it holds.

If you landed in the "I Need to Do More of It" category (2 to 3), you may choose to skip around, seeking to focus on areas where you have the greatest gaps.

If your overall score reflects that you "Do It Consistently" (3), congratulations! Challenge yourself by thinking of different contexts or scenarios where your skills may be tested further or where you want to apply your talents more deliberately.

We encourage you to practice the concepts in the chapters, not just read them. Each chapter contains activities alongside stories, frameworks, and tips. Remember, facilitation excellence is a set of skills. The more you practice, the more adept and effective you will become. And the more impact — and fulfillment — you will achieve.

Here we go!

2. Manage Yourself

Nurtures overall well-being and healthy mindsets

I maintain my energy and health.

I am aware of my personal triggers and have strategies to manage them.

I am conscious of bias and have tools to minimize it.

I recognize and address my unsupportive self-talk.

The day Yasmin was scheduled to lead a kickoff meeting with a new client, she was jolted awake by her alarm. She hadn't slept well. That was not unusual; caring for an elderly parent and fourteen-year-old twins, and supporting a partner who traveled often, meant she found herself staying up late to catch up on work, managing other people's schedules, or simply try to decompress. When she did get to bed, she often slept fitfully, worrying about everything and everyone she needed to support.

Because she had been recently promoted, this kickoff meeting represented her first time to be leading solo. Adding to the pressure, the group consisted solely of high-powered senior executives. Her thoughts raced as she got her kids to the bus stop and made sure her mom was settled with breakfast before the Zoom call was to begin. *What if I'm not ready for this? If it doesn't go well, it will be my fault.* Yasmin skipped breakfast. Who has time for that? As she dialed into the call, her next thought was *Don't screw up.*

Yasmin's nervousness showed from the start. Her voice shook, and she spoke fast, making little eye contact and jumping right into the presentation. It got awkward quickly when the senior leaders picked up on and reacted to her nervousness. Some started to look at their phones, others stayed silent. One person interrupted several times and asked a question that poked at her credibility. When the meeting ended, Yasmin felt disappointed. She thought, *I knew it wasn't going to go well.*

Perhaps you identify with Yasmin. Most of us have had experiences when we feel especially nervous or things do not go as we hoped. Typically, when we look back and try to learn from these moments, we focus on them as isolated incidents. While there is plenty to glean from reflecting on a specific situation, recognizing and addressing our larger self-ecosystem of well-being and awareness can prove just as valuable.

To maximize our impact, the first people we need to be able to support and guide is ourselves. Without conscious awareness of our habits, triggers, biases, and self-talk, we can easily become passengers in our own experiences and have misalignment between our intentions and our impact.

Much of what we talk about in this book involves choices we make in the moment while we are engaged with others — but just as an athlete does, great facilitators recognize that the capacity to show up in good form on game day requires ongoing attention and care every day of the year. Let's break down the areas that deserve our attention and support.

Manage Your Well-being

Leading with impact requires that we feel fit and well. There are many dimensions to wellness and many scales to identify and measure those dimensions.[2,3,4,5]

 Physical wellness: Our body-based healt. Supporting our physical health involves getting enough rest, in terms of both sleep and taking breaks from activity, eating well, exercising, and — of course — treating or managing any physical problems. Our friend Yasmin, in the story above, was sleep-deprived, which could contribute to her inability to react quickly and think clearly.

 Emotional wellness: A healthy balance of positive emotional states. Although some facilitators focus on "good" emotions in this category, others identify emotional wellness more in terms of emotional self-awareness and resilience.

2 UMatter Princeton University. https://umatter.princeton.edu/action/caring-yourself/wellness-wheel-assessment#Princeton-UMatter-Wellness-Self-Assessment
3 Lee, M.T., Weziak-Bialowolska, D., Mooney, K.D., Lerner, P.J., McNeely, E., Vander-Weele, T.J. (2020). Self-assessed importance of domains of flourishing: demographics and correlations with well-being. Journal of Positive Psychology, in press.
4 Loehr, Jim and Schwartz, Tony The Power of Full Engagement, Free Press, Jan, 2005
5 Seligman, Martin, The Pursuit of Happiness https://www.pursuit-of-happiness.org/history-of-happiness/martin-seligman-psychology/

Social wellness: Possessing a healthy network of support and care, feeling a genuine sense of connection with key individual relationships and a sense of belonging and community. Yasmin was flying solo for the first time in the story above. Did she feel like she could reach out to her peers, her leader, or a mentor for help in the meeting?

 Intellectual/mental wellness: The ability to focus, learn, and feel stimulated creatively. This category includes both the capacity to concentrate and a sense of interest, fulfillment, and meaning from our cognitive activities. Yasmin put a great deal of stress on herself to "not screw up." By holding herself up to impossibly high standards, she limits her ability to stay curious and learn and grow.

 Spiritual wellness or purpose: Holding values, beliefs, and intentions that give meaning and purpose to life, and the opportunity to act in alignment with them. For example, Yasmin, who may be the primary earner in her family, might feel constrained because she feels as if she is working solely for a paycheck rather than finding fulfillment in her job. This limitation could hinder her ability to express fully herself and engage with her responsibilities.

Some wellness researchers include additional categories like financial wellness and occupational or environmental wellness (using resources responsibly and creating healthy environments for others). However, these categories are often rolled into the ones above.

We can become depleted in any one of these areas, and when we are, it is hard to maintain our motivation and productivity. Use this exercise to take a moment to assess your current wellness state.

My Current Well-being

As you review your assessment, where do you see opportunities to increase your health and wellness so you can show up at your best, with all the energy, focus, and presence that leading requires? Addressing how to improve in each of these areas goes beyond the scope of this book, but once you have identified places where you might want to make shifts, myriad resources are available.

Here are three areas to begin with.

1. Identify the area of well-being that will have the greatest return on your investment. This may or may not be your lowest score from the exercise. For example, maybe you are not sleeping or eating well because you feel out of alignment with your purpose, or you have just relocated and feel lonely and unmoored. Ask yourself not only which area of focus might have the most long-term impact but which feels easiest to address right away.

2. Choose one small action to take to affect this area. Tiny shifts like these could have positive effects:

- Take a walk at lunch rather than eating at your desk.

- Turn off screens 30 minutes before bedtime.

- Eat healthier.

- Watch a funny movie or go see an improv show.

- Call a friend.

- Meditate or simply breathe.

- Create a vision statement or vision board.

- Take a course/learn a new skill.

- Start keeping, or being better about making entries in, a journal.

- Schedule a difficult conversation that you've been avoiding.

- Make an appointment to review current medications with your healthcare provider. You never know what side effects might be affecting you. *(After years of taking the migraine medication Topamax, Kat discovered it went by the nickname "dopamax" because doctors knew it caused cognitive impairment. Weaning herself off that drug transformed her well-being in many areas.)*

3. Track the impact of your shifts. Are you feeling better? What areas of well-being have been affected? How could you adjust your behavior to more fully apply what's working?

Targeting specific ways to increase your energy and well-being will, by definition, allow you to show up with more to give. The ubiquitous advice to "put your own oxygen mask on first" holds especially true for anyone who wishes to lead a group effectively. In other words, investing in your own well-being will pay dividends.

Manage Hot Buttons

When things are going smoothly and we are at our best, the skills and mindsets discussed here can feel accessible, even easy. But when something hijacks our rationality and calmness, behaving in alignment with our values and intentions gets harder. When we get activated, we are literally flooded with chemicals and use more primitive parts of our brain. Our cognitive functions become impaired, and we experience what is known as "amygdala hijack."

Behaving in facilitator mode requires us to anticipate what might trigger us so we can inoculate ourselves (to whatever extent possible). We all have hot buttons that can sabotage us; knowing what they are and having strategies for managing them goes a long way toward defanging them.

Know your hot buttons. Types of triggering activations range from specific words or comments to emotional states to physical sensations to sights and sounds. They can arise from past experiences, values, and beliefs; style preferences; ego protection; or physical sensitivities. Regardless of where they come from, the best time to identify them is *before* they arise and hobble us.

Casey, for example, knows that she tends to get defensive when people in her training push back on the methodology she is using or ask her to cite more evidence of its value. Cole can't stand the sound of chewing. Jenna hates being called "dear" or "honey." Martine is strongly invested in social justice issues and deeply bothered by language that appears exclusionary or biased.

Although these stimuli seem wildly different, each has the power to knock the triggered person off balance, even though the behavior may seem neutral or even potentially positive to someone who isn't triggered.

What's the big deal with asking to cite the source? Chewing is necessary, so how else are we supposed to eat? "Dear" is a term of endearment — who wouldn't like that? The point is not to judge your triggers as valid or invalid, or to try to change them. Simply being aware of them is the name of the game at this stage.

Most of us can easily identify certain activating topics or scenarios, whereas others remain murky or unrecognized. But the more of ours we can discover, the less often we will be caught off guard and out of control.

This process should help.

 Identify what activates you. Think back to moments when you felt physically or emotionally hijacked. Consider what happened right before. Try to identify, as specifically as possible, the behaviors, sights, and sounds. Write down any hot buttons you identify.

 Recognize your reactions. Once you know them, turn your attention to what happens when those stimuli arise. You are almost certainly familiar with the colloquial stress response phrase "fight or flight," originally described by Harvard Medical School physiologist Walter Bradford Cannon in 1915. Current research[6] suggests that there are four or more fear responses: fight, flee, freeze, and fawn. (Some frameworks add fainting as well, which is full collapse, like a possum playing dead, but others consider this a subset of freezing.)

In the world of facilitation, these behavioral responses show up like this:

 Fight: getting aggressive or defensive; debating or attacking others

 Flight: avoiding topics, not addressing disruptive behavior; failing to lead when direction is necessary; redirecting away from important but uncomfortable interactions

---

6 Bracha. H. Stefan "Freeze, Flight, Fight, Fright, Faint: Adaptationist Perspectives on the Acute Stress Response Spectrum" , CNS Spectrums, September 2004

Freeze: shutting down; feeling unable to listen or articulate your point of view; getting stuck or indecisive about where to go next

 Fawn: acquiescing to people with power and status; providing disingenuous positive feedback

The intensity and type of response a person has can vary depending on the context and intensity of the trigger, but many have habitual ways of dealing with our most common triggers. In the world of improvisational theater, for example, some improvisers tend to fight for control of a scene when they are stressed. Others flee or freeze. Think about yourself: What are your typical behaviors under stress?

Think of a moment in conversation or when leading a meeting when one of your identified triggers happened. Recall how you reacted. Can you identify which type of response you had? Think of other similar moments. Do you notice a pattern?

Knowing your tendencies can help you balance them: If you tend to fight for control, practice pausing, offering less, and focusing on accepting what your partners say and do. If you freeze, on the other hand, work on sharing your voices and jumping in more assertively. Regardless of your instinctive reaction, some general approaches can help you manage your stress response before or during an event:

 Prepare: Once we know our hot buttons, we can often anticipate them. What might you put in place to avoid or minimize the likelihood of those

occurring? For example, establishing behavior agreements at the beginning of a meeting and even sharing known hot buttons can help you and others show up in ways that make them less likely to happen. You might be able to ask, for instance, that participants use low or soft voices to express critiques or ask questions.

 Be mindful: Pay attention to your body. A mentor of Kat's used to say, "It's easier to change your body than to change your mind." Noticing what is happening to you physically pulls you into the present and helps you recognize that you have been triggered. Notice your emotions. Notice your thoughts.

 Pause: Start by breathing. If necessary, and your reaction is severe, give yourself a break. Continuing in an activated state will have more severe consequences than asking for a moment to collect yourself.

 Manage the stories in your head: Separate what is observably true from what is a story you are making up. (More on that in Chapter 7, Engage with Story)

 Check in; get curious: Others may be activated as well; ask if anyone is feeling uncomfortable or knows about catalysts that could affect their ability to participate fully. Keeping an open mind and understanding other people's reactions can both interrupt the physical symptoms of being triggered and defuse your negative emotions and the stories in your head.

Prepare

Looking ahead can help defuse your reaction to triggers. Think about an upcoming engagement.

 What can you anticipate that might be difficult or activating? What guardrails or agreements could you put in place proactively to diminish the likelihood of such concerns?

 What strategies do you want to have at the ready if you do get activated?

 Review past moments to identify what has helped you.

 What can you recognize as hot buttons for others? How can you focus on supporting them when they are activated?

Manage Bias

Kat introduced a group activity exactly as she had done dozens of times, choosing her words deliberately, with what she thought was sensitivity and awareness. The activity was designed to create awareness and respect for differences, and communication gaps.

"You're going to divide into pairs," she said. "One of you is from today; the other is from 300 years ago. Lots of different things were happening in the world 300 years ago, but around here, the culture was mostly agrarian. And the most important thing is we had not yet harnessed electricity for daily use."

She ran the activity as usual, and it seemed to go just fine. At the end of the day, one person approached her. "I need to give you some feedback on that activity," they said. "When you said 'think back to 300 years ago,' what was happening for my people was slavery. That agrarian culture you highlighted was plantations where my relatives were forced to work."

As soon as she heard the feedback, Kat saw how clearly problematic her setup had been. In fact, she had trouble figuring out how she could have missed this obvious association. In trying to acknowledge that not all cultures were homogenous 300 years ago, she had inadvertently underscored historical trauma.

But she had not noticed this on her own; it took someone having had the courage to point it out for her to become aware — and reset her introduction. Before this moment, Kat had always considered the 300-year conversation exercise one of her slam-dunk, surest-to-succeed activities. If she had missed this unintended impact, what else was she missing?

Managing bias is a much deeper, broader topic than we can address here fully. Fortunately, there are more and more wonderful resources available every day. That said, it is imperative to recognize you will have biases, so put guardrails in place to manage them.

Here are some high-level steps to support that process.

Search yourself. Start by distinguishing some terms. For our purposes, a bias is an attribution or preference that interferes with impartial judgment. Bias could be in favor or against someone or something, and might or might not involve prejudice (a premature judgment or opinion about others before gaining sufficient knowledge or as a result of selectively disregarding facts), or discrimination (an action taken toward members of a group based on prejudice that denies justice, resources, and fair treatment of people and groups).

In some places, like the U.S., the topic of bias has become highly politicized, but make no mistake: Everyone has biases. To say one is unbiased is the same as saying, "I have no preferences, habits, cultural experiences, or attitudes." Because we live in systems that are discriminatory and unequal, recognizing our biases can bring up feelings of defensiveness, shame, and guilt. But only when we allow ourselves to acknowledge that we have biases can we expand our awareness of other people's experiences, and test our assumptions and narratives so we can serve others and achieve our facilitative goals.

Educate yourself. Although we cannot eliminate our biases completely, we can expand our awareness of common cultural or systemic biases to which we might be falling prey. In the U.S., for example, we tend to favor extraversion over introversion, conflating it with confidence, charisma, and leadership capacity. Of course, we also have embedded racial biases that continue to cause significant issues for individuals and our culture at large. To that point, let us be very clear: Not all biases are created equal. A bias in favor of chocolate ice cream over other flavors is not the same as a bias in favor of male or white leaders over females or people of color.

Fortunately, there's an increasing amount of research and clear-eyed texts addressing the specific, common biases; the process of bias; and how to counteract it. For those committed to consistently identifying and challenging their biases, it's essential to seek knowledge and insights as a regular practice. We are never done with expanding our awareness. Culture is dynamic, and humans are complex. There is always more to learn.

Connect with others. More books, videos, and podcasts on these topics become available every day. And an important source of information is the humans you interact with. The participant in Kat's workshop was able to offer insight that Kat missed, even though Kat thought she had been connected to the most up-to-date thinking on the topic. Context influences which biases show up in meaningful ways, so checking in with others about their assumptions and experiences can uncover important blind spots or missteps.

Therese, for example, remembers a time in Singapore when she was recording colleagues' initials on a flipchart to divide the work. One person's name was Wei Chen, so Therese wrote "WC." The room erupted in laughter. WC in many countries denotes a toilet (water closet). The colleague was embarrassed, and, of course, so was Therese. No ill intention, of course; simply an innocent blind spot. But Therese remembers the incident much more vividly than any general information about bias she might have read in a book.

A note here: Those of us in positions of privilege (read, members of a dominant culture or in an empowered position) may, with the best of intentions, ask others to engage in the labor of educating us. This is not what we are suggesting. We must all take responsibility for our own learning, especially in areas that might be triggering for others. Opening yourself to others' preferences and context can be an important source of development. Had Therese heard laughter and simply ignored it, she might have lost the group's trust, and she certainly would have missed out on an opportunity to learn. Instead, by getting curious and asking what had caused that reaction, she was able to gain insight and repair.

Set agreements. Knowing that bias always exists in a system, we can create ground rules and agreements at the beginning of interactions that will support positive interaction. One example we like is to "assume positive intent and take responsibility for your impact." Typically, a facilitator might offer the first half of this suggestion, "assume positive intent" to groups, and it can sound and feel good. Who wouldn't want to assume positive intent? But this statement itself may have embedded bias.

When we hurt or offend others, intent is important. If someone inadvertently bumps into you and spills their coffee, you will react very differently than if you think they deliberately threw a cup of coffee at you. But regardless of the intent, if the coffee is hot, you may still get burned and injured. If the owner of the coffee responded to your cries of pain by saying, "I didn't do it on purpose; get over it," that would feel both inappropriate and heartless. However, if you find yourself accidentally spilling coffee on folks regularly (even if your intent was good), perhaps you need to examine how you are carrying your mug and claiming space, as well as how aware you are of others around you. Intent constitutes only part of the interpersonal equation.

Acknowledge harm and repair. Because we all have biases and even our best intentions sometimes do not align with our impact, we will say or do things that could hurt others. How we respond when we become aware that we have disturbed someone else matters at least as much as the initial action.

To repair, seek to understand before you seek to be understood. In other words, the necessary first part of fixing any mistake is to be open to hearing what went wrong.

Manage Bias

Ask yourself:

 How can I diversify and vet my sources of information?

 How can I research and challenge my assumptions and beliefs?

 How can I build education regarding bias into my general practices?

 What agreements and disclosures should I put in place ahead of time?

 How can I remain open to feedback and sharing when I have transgressed?

Manage Self-Talk

We talk to ourselves all the time, even when we're not aware of it, and that inner voice can hinder or help us. When we cultivate it, our self-talk can guide and support us through life. When it's not serving us well, it's our inner critic, the troll on our shoulder, that is second-guessing and censoring us.

Self-talk helps us navigate through life. It aids in memory[7] and recall. Think about how you silently repeat a phone number or an address so you don't forget it. Our inner voice aids in cognition and performance.[8] We quietly talk ourselves through a math problem, plan our day while in the shower or heading into a meeting, and repeat an encouraging phrase to ourselves. Professional athletes know that their internal dialogue can often be the difference between a winning or disappointing performance. Research[9] supports that our internal voice is up to three times faster than verbal communication. You can say a lot of negative or positive things to yourself in seconds.

The point isn't to try to mute that inner voice. A better approach is to be aware of it, then manage it in support of our objectives and goals. Turning up the volume on supportive voices will help us while turning down the internal critic hindering us.

---

7 Lupyan, G., & Swingley, D. (2012). Self-Directed Speech Affects Visual Search Per-formance. Quarterly Journal of Experimental Psychology, 65(6), 1068–1085. https://doi.org/10.1080/17470218.2011.647039.

8 Neck, C.,& Manz, C. (1992). Thought self-leadership: The influence of self-talk and mental imagery on performance. Journal of Organizational Behavior, Vol. 13, 681–699.

9 Korba, R. J. (1990). The Rate of Inner Speech. Perceptual and Motor Skills, 71(3), 1043–1052. https://doi.org/10.2466/pms.1990.71.3.1043.

Become Aware of Your Inner Voice

Awareness begins with paying attention to what you are thinking or feeling at any moment. As you meet with your boss, are you noticing tension in your shoulders? Are you clenching your jaw or breathing steadily and feeling relaxed? Our physical and emotional reactions can be our first clue to what we're saying to ourselves. Sometimes our self-talk starts as a feeling and not words. Other times, we're more aware of different voices in our heads that are not our own — a mentor who inspired or encouraged us, a parent who is a constant cheerleader, or a boss who was critical of our performance.

To become more consciously aware of your inner voice, try these practices:

 Be still. When we're constantly in motion and rushed, it's easier to ignore or overlook what we're saying to ourselves. Find a quiet moment in your day and become aware of all the thoughts entering your mind. See how many thoughts you can notice.

 Be neutral. Allow yourself to have thoughts without initially judging or dismissing them.

 Be curious. Ask yourself, why am I thinking this thought? What's surprising me? Is that thought helping me or getting in my way?

The Self-Talk Cycle

Once you are aware of your inner voice, you're better positioned to understand how it's affecting you.

Remember Yasmin's self-talk at the start of this chapter? It was *Don't screw up*. That thought made her nervous, anxious, and unsure. Those feelings affected her behaviors (for example, no eye contact, no questions to the group, and talking fast) and led to an uncomfortable meeting — in part because of what she was saying to herself. Our self-talk is like a self-fulfilling prophecy, and we're usually not consciously aware of its effect on us. Our thoughts drive our emotions, which affect our behaviors. Then others react and respond to our behaviors. This graphic show how it works.

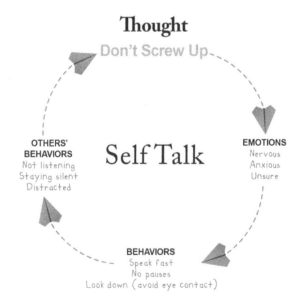

Self-talk doesn't just apply to imposter-syndrome thinking — when we don't believe our success is deserved or we underestimate our abilities. Kat and Therese have worked with loads of leaders who are overconfident and not self-aware. They suffer similar negative outcomes when they don't manage their self-talk. Left unchecked, their reactions may sound like overconfidence:

- *I've heard this all before.*
- *I know more than they do.*
- *It's not a big deal.*

Thought
I've heard this all before

OTHERS' BEHAVIORS
Rush their message
Stop talking
Withhold information

Self Talk

EMOTIONS
Impatient
Frustrated
Annoyed

BEHAVIORS
Interrupt
Don't ask questions
Stop listening

The Dunning Krueger Effect[10] describes how we tend to overestimate our abilities or skills. Ironically, when we are

---

10 Kruger, Justin and Dunning, David (1999) "Unskilled and unaware of it: how difficulties in recognizing one's own incompetence lead to inflated self-assessments." Journal of Personality and social Psychology 77 6: 112134 .

the least competent, we might feel the most confident. Imagine someone who thinks they are a skilled presenter. When no one asks a question, they think to themselves *Wow. No questions must mean I'm really good at this!* Without appropriate feedback, we don't get the internal warning signals that prompt us to question our thinking or be curious. Your presentation might have been quite thorough, but no questions might mean you've offended, confused, or bored your audience.

The good news is that we can switch tone and content so the voice in our head can help us accomplish a goal. We can speak to ourselves as an ally, a coach, and a problem solver, not just a saboteur. The trick is distinguishing which voices are which, then turning up the volume on the voice that will help us at the moment. These tables provide some guidance for figuring out those voices, and which ones to respond to.

WHO IS IN YOUR HEAD?	
Supportive (Helpful)	**Unsupportive (Not Helpful)**
The Internal Coach Focuses on the goal and your value. *Even if I'm not the expert, I have enough knowledge to contribute to this conversation*	**Overly Self-Assured** Over-inflates your knowledge or capability. *They don't have any questions, so they must like it.*
Objective Observer Focuses on being factual and unbiased *You've been talking for 10 minutes now. Stop and listen.*	**Fearful Overthinker** Feeds into self-doubt. *I'm bad at this. They aren't interested in what I have to say.*

Here's how to manage your self-talk.

Tune In

The chatter in our heads is constant. Sometimes it tells us benign things like *I'm hungry. It's cold today. Don't forget to pick up the dry cleaning.* Like a river over rocks, our chatter is constantly flowing. We're often not aware of what we're saying to ourselves, and we can glide through our day without the need to put effort into tuning into it. Yet in important moments, that internal voice can say things that get in our way, like *They're going to hate it. I've done this 100 times before. It's all the same* — and that's when it's important to manage our self-talk.

The first step is tuning into what you're saying to yourself and creating some psychological distance between you and the thought. The easiest way is to think about a strong emotion you felt recently (frustrated, anxious, confused, nervous, confident). Now ask yourself: *What am I saying to that's making me feel that way?* For instance, you worked with a quiet group, and you couldn't get a dialogue going. Your self-talk might be: *No matter what I do, I just get silence.* If you don't recognize that self-talk, it reinforces itself, and the nervousness increases. If you project your anxiety and tension onto people, they'll react to it. It's contagious.

Record

Because our thoughts can be like a runaway train, we can easily lose control over our ability to manage self-talk. To control your thoughts, write down what you're saying to yourself, especially before a big moment where you need to be at your best. Seeing your words on paper gives you more control over your thinking and allows you to be more objective and consider whether that self-talk will help or get in the way of your goal.

Gabe had to deliver news to his team about an organizational change. He disagreed with the decision and expected a lot of pushback and frustration from his team. As he wrestled with the news, the chatter in his head was *I have no choice. I'm just the messenger.* He jotted down his thinking, then considered what would happen in the meeting if it continued to rattle around in his head. He knew he would stumble through the announcement, deflect their frustration, and blame senior leadership — "Hey, don't shoot the messenger!" In essence, he wouldn't show up as a leader. Recording his thoughts gave him a moment to reflect and stop his mind from racing.

Reframe and Revise

By becoming more aware of the sound track in your head, you can change the message to something more supportive. The key is revising self-talk to something believable and supportive, not falsely positive. For instance, if Gabe thought *I'll be fine. Just get through it,* that probably wouldn't help him much. Instead, supportive self-talk might be: *It's not my decision, but I need to own the message to be seen as a leader or focus on helping the team see the bigger picture.*

When in doubt, try revising your self-talk to something that encourages curiosity, like *I wonder what it will take to get others to be open to hearing my idea?* Curious self-talk helps you stay more neutral and open to possibilities.

If you're anxious, reframe your self-talk to focus on your excitement. Harvard University professor Alison Wood Brooks conducted a study[11] to describe how anxiety and excitement are both high-arousal emotions. Both are controlled automatically by our nervous system, and it's not in our immediate control to shut them off. It's why simply telling yourself to calm down doesn't work. Rather than trying to lower your emotional state, it's more effective to reframe your thinking from *I'm anxious about having this conversation* to *I'm excited to find a solution we can both be happy with.*

Repeat

Unfortunately, it's not as simple as stating your revised self-talk once and magically never saying unhelpful things to yourself again. Learning to manage the voice in your head takes repetition. It needs to become a habit. It requires repeating the supportive self-talk and catching yourself when your inner critic tries to overrule you.

Sanjay was invited to the senior leadership meeting and had to announce a delay in a much-anticipated product launch. He tended to ramble when he was nervous, so he said to himself: *Go slow. Deliver the news clearly and*

11 Brooks, A. W. (2014) "Get Excited: Reappraising Pre-Performance Anxiety as Excitement." Journal of Experimental Psychology: General 143, no. 3 (June 2014): 1144–1158. (Received Outstanding Dissertation Award from International Association for Conflict Management 2013.)

concisely. During the meeting, as he was asked rapid-fire questions, he caught himself speaking quickly. He thought to himself: *Slow and steady.* That was enough to help him stay on track with his message.

Nerves are normal. Expect them to react. What's more important is your next thought after recognizing the nerves. Scolding yourself not to be nervous won't work. Instead, acknowledge the voice and repeat more supportive self-talk.

Try This: Manage Self Talk

- Think about an upcoming situation where you're feeling a strong emotion (nervous, anxious, worried, angry).

- Record what you're saying to yourself. Ask yourself, *Will that self-talk support me in achieving my goal?* If the answer is no, revise it.

- Reframe and Revise your self-talk to something that will support you and is believable.

- Repeat it. What will help you recall that message when you need it at the moment?

Manage Your Self-Talk	
Unsupportive	**Supportive**
"This is no big deal."	"It's important to them. Treat it with respect."
"I've done this a hundred times."	"This is new for them. Look at it through their eyes."
"This is going to be easy."	"Focus on what's unique in this situation."
"What if I mess up?"	"I've done similar things that are hard. No one is expecting perfection."
"They just won't listen."	"I wonder what it will take for them to hear a different point of view?"
"That will never work."	"Stay curious. What might I be missing?"
"We'll never reach agreement."	"This relationship is worth it. Listen for what they value."
"I'm not good at this."	"No one starts as an expert. I know I can learn to get good at it."
"I'm so nervous!"	"Nerves are normal. Breathe deeply."
"I should have prepared more."	"Focus on what you know."
"They don't agree with me."	"Pushback is normal. It's not personal."
"I'm boring them."	"They might be distracted but it doesn't mean they aren't interested."
"Why is this taking so long?"	"If people feel heard and understood, we can move faster."

Focus on Breath

Have you ever felt as if you were having an out-of-body experience during a stressful meeting or you just couldn't think straight? Then afterward, you replay it and think of all the eloquent gems you wish you could have said.

During stressful moments or when we are emotionally triggered, our bodies take over. Breathing becomes rapid and shallow. Heart rate increases. Palms sweat. Stomach gets upset. Those physical reactions are the result of the hardwiring in the brain activating the fight-or-flight response discussed earlier. Your sympathetic nervous system can't tell the difference between a saber tooth tiger and your boss putting you on the spot about why you can't add more to your workload.

The rational, thinking part of our brain — the prefrontal cortex — becomes impaired when we're stressed.[12] As a result, it's hard to think clearly and respond well, but with breathing techniques, it is possible to gain some mastery over our mind.

Becoming aware of how your body is reacting is the first step to centering yourself and managing the moment. When we control our breath, we regulate our nervous system and are more capable at managing the stressors. Research[13] shows that changing our breathing can change how we feel.

Purposeful deep breathing allows you to calm yourself and increase your attention span[14] to focus on the speaker. You'll be in a better state of mind to respond thoughtfully.

12 Schaeuble, Derek et al, (2019) Prefrontal Cortex Regulates Chronic Stress-Induced Cardiovascular Susceptibility; Journal of the American Heart Association, Vol 8, No. 4.
13 Pierre Philippot, Gaëtane Chapelle, and Sylvie Blairy (2002). Respiratory feedback in the generation of emotion, Cognition and Emotion, 16:5, 605-627, DOI: 10.1080/02699930143000392.
14 Ma X, Yue ZQ, Gong ZQ, Zhang H, Duan NY, Shi YT, Wei GX, and Li YF. The Effect of Diaphragmatic Breathing on Attention, Negative Affect and Stress in Healthy Adults. Front Psychol. (2017) Jun 6;8:874. doi: 10.3389/fpsyg.2017.00874. PMID: 28626434; PMCID: PMC5455070.

Here's how this technique[15] works:

 Get in a comfortable position.

 Put a hand on your torso below your ribs and the other hand on your chest.

 Breathe in deeply through your nose to the count of four and out through your mouth, silently counting to four.

 As you breathe in, feel your chest rise with air. Then, feel your chest lower as you exhale. Take three more full, deep breaths.

Verbalize Your Thinking

When it seems impossible to get the voice in your head under control, find a friend. Sharing the chatter in your head (especially feelings[16]) with someone you trust can help generate new, supportive thinking.

Byron was early in his career and just finished a special high-profile project. He was invited to present at the company's quarterly meeting, attended by the top senior leaders. At first, he was thrilled. What an honor and great exposure. As the big day drew near, though, that excitement turned to trepidation and fear.

15 Riehl, Megan, Psy.D (2016, May 17) An Easier Way to Beat Stress – And Build a Healthier Life [Blog post]; MichiganMedicine.org
16 Matthew D. Lieberman, Naomi I. Eisenberger, Molly J. Crockett, Sabrina M. Tom, Jennifer H. Pfeifer, and Baldwin M. Way (2007) Putting Feelings Into Words Affect Labeling Disrupts Amygdala Activity in Response to Affective Stimuli, Psychological Science; University of California, Los Angeles.

Byron went to his mentor, Malika. He divulged his thinking: "I'm really excited for this opportunity, but I'm also petrified. I've never done this kind of project before. I'm definitely not an expert. They'll see through this. Help me get my head on straight."

Malika smiled and said, "It's understandable to be nervous. It's a big moment in front of a lot of influential people." Then she asked, "Do you think they expect you to have all the answers?"

He replied, "Well, they want to highlight this project because it went really well."

Malika said, "OK, so you have a good news story to share."

"Yes, but what if they ask me a question and I freeze or look bad, or say the wrong thing, or, or, or — ," said Byron.

"That's a lot of what ifs, Byron! No one is expecting you to be perfect."

Byron was silent and reflective. "I know. I know. Maybe I should just concentrate on telling my story about this project. After all, it is my story, and if I get asked a question, I probably know where to go to get the answers."

"That's right! Tell it from your perspective," Malika replied.

"OK, that's helpful, Malika. I just have to concentrate on telling my story."

On the day of the big event, Byron was a blend of excitement and nerves. As he walked to the podium, he quietly took a deep breath and repeated to himself: *Just tell your story. Just tell your story.* As a result of managing his self-talk, he smiled, spoke clearly and concisely, and managed his rate of speech.

The bottom line is, if you don't manage your self-talk, it will manage you.

Chapter Takeaways

- Nurture overall well-being by regularly checking your health, focusing on energy and presence for effective leadership, and identifying the well-being area with the highest return on investment.

- Identify hot buttons by recognizing words, emotions, physical sensations, or past experiences that trigger a response in you. Interrupt those automatic reactions by managing internal narratives, pausing in the moment, and seeking input from others.

- Manage bias by educating yourself about common, cultural, and systemic biases, while consistently questioning assumptions, diversifying information sources, and remaining open to feedback.

- Distinguish between supportive and unsupportive self-talk. Amplify the voice that will be most helpful in the moment.

- Effectively manage self-talk by first recognizing what you're saying to yourself. Then record your thoughts to gain control and objectivity, revise the thoughts in your head to be supportive and believable, and repeat these steps to solidify the new thought processes.

3. Model Values and Beliefs

Align actions and words with principles

I have identified my core values and beliefs.

My behaviors align with my values and beliefs.

I work to understand others' values and beliefs.

I take others' beliefs and values into account when interacting.

Alvin Toffler, after graduating from New York University in 1950 with a degree in English, embarked on a surprising path. He and his new wife, Heidi, moved to Cleveland, Ohio, where they became factory workers on assembly lines — work they would engage in for the next five years. As activists interested in the lives and needs of workers, the Tofflers wanted to experience the life of an American industrial worker firsthand, not just read or theorize about it.

At various points in their journey, Heidi worked in and served as the union shop steward in an aluminum foundry. Alvin took on jobs as a millwright and welder.

The Tofflers would go on to collaborate on a number of influential works, most famous among them the books *Future Shock* and *The Third Wave*, which introduced countless new ideas and phrases into our lexicon including *prosumer* and *information overload*.

In her 2016 article celebrating Alvin Toffler's life, Deb Westphal shared the core values of Toffler Associates, the advisory consultancy the Tofflers started. They are:

 Engage in diversity and give in to curiosity.

 Make a commitment to connect.

 Speak truth to power.

 Be a lifelong learner.

From the very start of their careers, we can see how the Tofflers lived their values.

The task of identifying and expressing values, which companies frequently undertake, can become monotonous and detached, often leading to widespread cynicism. But at heart, from Confucius to Aristotle to Angela Davis, we find questions of values and ethics infinitely compelling and complex. Nothing could be more important than determining what we most deeply believe and care about. As we begin to engage as facilitators, building our moral compass enables us to employ all the other tools and mindsets with intention and positive impact. They guide *how* we will get to a destination as much as they inform *where* we intend to go.

A facilitation case in point: Kat was approached by one of the Big 4 consulting firms to deliver a version of these facilitation skills virtually for their senior partners. The major contract arrived after some other projects had recently fallen through. It felt as if Kat's business might just hang in the balance.

Working with people on the global strategy team, Kat designed a customized series of three ninety-minute sessions that she would deliver three times, each spaced a couple of hours apart to accommodate three time zones each week. A huge amount of thought and planning went into designing the most effective and appropriate version of the material for this particular audience in this context, aligning with the larger initiatives, cultures, unique historic moment, and programmatic goals.

Then the first delivery happened.

By the time Kat had led this group through the program, she clearly felt that the sessions as designed missed the mark in some fundamental ways — but she felt certain she knew what to do to make them more effective at meeting the stated goals. She did wonder whether, after all the vetting and planning, she could change things on the fly. Making significant adjustments after all that work and without the chance to connect with her high-powered and impressive clients felt risky. Would they get annoyed that she had done so without permission? Would her instinct for what would work better actually succeed? Would she be able to pull off the redesign in the moment with no time to prepare or rehearse?

Kat's first impulse was to play it safe: No one could blame her for sticking with the plan. But she realized one of her core values was at stake: adaptability. If, in fact, she truly believed that excellent facilitation meant modifying the plan to suit the needs of the moment, how could she *not* make the shift? This is the thing about values: They only really get tested when stakes are high.

What Is a Value?

In an environment of commodifying the identification and promoting of value statements, we can lose the essence of what a value is. Unfortunately, many folks who do "values"work in organizations simply provide a laundry list of words or cards with images and have people pick their favorites in the moment. Although the opportunity for self-reflection can always reap rewards, true values work that leads to lasting, robust understanding deserves deeper engagement.

What do we mean by the words we choose? What are words we simply like versus beliefs we hold or ethical standards we hold ourselves to? What do we feel obligated to profess versus what do we actually care about? What even *is* a value?

The American Psychological Association defines a value as "a moral, social, or aesthetic principle accepted by an individual or society as a guide to what is good, desirable, or important."

Many values frameworks exist with various areas of focus and utility for our context. Shalom H. Schwartz, Milton Rokeach, Florence Kluckhohn, and Fred Strodtbeck, to name a few thought leaders, have offered frameworks of varying complexity and universality, enumerating sets of universal values from six to thirty-six. Regardless of the number they use, many values researchers share the idea that there are relevant cross-cultural core principles and ethical dimensions. Fundamentally, we are all simply human.

Each of these thinkers brings unique insights that can help us explore our own values and how they align with the values of the groups we interact with.

Identifying Values

Milton Rokeach, the social psychologist, dominated the field for many years with the Rokeach Value Survey, introduced in his 1968 book, *Beliefs, Attitudes and Values*. In his subsequent work, *The Nature of Human Values*, he further explored instrumental and terminal values. Although more recent studies have questioned Rokeach's thirty-six identified values, his concept of instrumental and terminal values has had a significant impact on the practice of values work and can help illuminate what really matters to us versus what behaviors we engage in merely as means to an end.

Terminal values are those we care about for their own sake. For instance, happiness: It's often pursued as an end goal. Instrumental values serve as a means to an end. For example, hard work is an instrumental value because it's often assumed to result in financial success. Rokeach labeled the values on his list as inherently terminal or instrumental. Other researchers[17] have questioned the validity of this construct. But regardless of whether a value is *always* terminal or instrumental, the distinction helps us discern what truly matters to us and distinguishes it from behaviors we may engage in solely as a means to achieve certain ends.

---

17 Heath, R. L., and Fogel, D. S. (1978). Terminal and Instrumental? An Inquiry into Rokeach's Value Survey. *Psychological Reports* 42(3_suppl), 1147-1154.

Rokeach's original list

TERMINAL VALUES	INSTRUMENTAL VALUES
• True Friendship	• Cheerfulness
• Mature Love	• Ambition
• Self-Respect	• Love
• Happiness	• Cleanliness
• Inner Harmony	• Self-Control
• Equality	• Capability
• Freedom	• Courage
• Pleasure	• Politeness
• Social Recognition	• Honesty
• Wisdom	• Imagination
• Salvation	• Independence
• Family Security	• Intellect
• National Security	• Broad-Mindedness
• A Sense of Accomplishment	• Logic
• A World of Beauty	• Obedience
• A World at Peace	• Helpfulness
• A Comfortable Life	• Responsibility
• An Exciting Life	• Forgiveness

Defining Belief or Beliefs

All right, we have defined values. Now, what's a belief? A belief is simply a tenet or conviction that you hold to be true. Why is it important to define belief? As facilitators, we must recognize that we do not enter the room as neutral blank slates. We have ideas and opinions. We have filters and biases, for better or worse. Knowing, investigating, and then owning our beliefs enables us to show up as clear and trustworthy stewards.

The Three Steps to Modeling Values and Beliefs

Having defined our terms, we can proceed to dive into the importance of identifying and modeling our beliefs and values. We focus here on where our personal values most support and influence our work as facilitators, but of course, the process holds for any situation you find yourself in. There are three steps to successfully modeling your values and beliefs:

1. Identify your relevant values and beliefs.

2. Pinpoint the specific behaviors and approaches that align with those values.

3. Walk the talk.

Step 1: Identify Your Relevant Values and Beliefs

In any given moment, facilitators face myriad choices. If we have identified our core relevant values ahead of time, they can act as a compass pointing toward the choice that will not only help us meet our goals, but help us create the kind of relationships and environments we desire.

Why do we say *relevant* values and beliefs? We hope you are always acting in alignment with your core human values and beliefs. As a facilitator, specifically, though, some of these will matter to your choices in the room more than others. For example, Kat has a general belief that everyone deserves to be seen and heard. It has informed her personal and professional choices in countless ways, most obviously in leading her to become a speaker coach and communication skills consultant. It has also affected her parenting, political, and volunteer activities. Clearly, though, this is a value that is relevant and helpful as a facilitator. She has another belief that eating a plant-based diet is an easy, healthy, and effective way to combat climate change. This may not show up as relevant quite as frequently in facilitation (although it might affect catering choices).

The kinds of questions to ponder to surface your facilitation values and beliefs include:

 What do you care about most in your interactions?

 What feels most important when you engage in conversations, lead meetings, and present?

 How do you want others to feel in your presence?

 What allows you to connect with individuals and teams?

 What motivates you to act as a facilitator in this context?

 How do you want to be perceived by others?

 What are your non-negotiables when leading conversations and groups?

 What do you stand for?

When you reflect on these questions, values may immediately spring to mind such as respect, expertise, or trust. Or certain beliefs: "Disagreement adds value." "Efficiency is next to godliness!" "Perfection is underrated."

Therese was coaching a newly appointed executive who held risk-taking as a core personal value. The company brought him on board to navigate rapidly changing market conditions and drive innovation. Taking calculated risks was essential for growth and competitiveness. He saw failure as a necessary step for growth. During team meetings, he demonstrated this value by encouraging his team to bring fresh ideas and prototype ideas rapidly. This style was in stark contrast to his predecessor, who valued correctness and adherence to processes, which often led to finger-pointing when mistakes were made.

Here are some examples of relevant beliefs a facilitator leading a training might have:

 Learning happens within the learner.

 When people feel powerful and capable, they learn and grow.

 I'm still learning.

In an early iteration of the facilitation framework, we called it "demonstrate beliefs" and we listed the three beliefs above as the beliefs that facilitators should embody.

"Learning happens within the learner" reminds us not to force-feed participants our content. When we train, we present material as well as we can and respect the learner's own process and openness to it. We provide experiences that allow people to apply and test concepts for themselves. If someone

resists or rejects a framework or idea, we seek to clarify confusion or answer questions, but we refrain from debating or insisting on the value of our offers.

The belief that "When people feel powerful and capable, they learn and grow" leads us to stay conscious of the status dynamics in the room (see the Establish Presence chapter) and seek opportunities to have participants tap into their own existing knowledge and expertise. We catch people progressing in the moment as they try new skills, and we encourage "Yes, and" questions and comments, even those that may seem adversarial or obstructionist (see the "Serve the Purpose" and "Balance Risk and Safety chapters). By highlighting the ways in which the learners are already succeeding, we help them feel confident and competent so they are willing to be more vulnerable, take more risks, and take on even more new challenges.

By embodying the belief, "I'm still learning," we stay curious and open ourselves, which sets the foundation for all of the other contributions. We listen with more interest; we adapt more readily; we create more safety and share more relevant information about not just the results but the process of learning. By remembering that we are one of the learners in the room and not some other, rarefied creature (separate, distant, and fully enlightened), we are able to empathize and understand others in the room more fully, and offer what they need more effectively. Oh, and of course, we also benefit by actually learning and growing ourselves — it's not just something we *say*.

At some point in our work, we realized that as useful as these three belief statements might prove, putting them above other possible values did a disservice to our trainees. We recognized that these were *our* beliefs but our clients had an even wider set of beliefs. We found ourselves customizing this contribution for each individual organizational culture and environment. Some of our clients' beliefs aligned with ours and were simply stated differently: "Everyone in the room has a voice, and we are all better for hearing it." Others articulated beliefs that strayed further from our central ones: "Working with intensity is a requirement to be best in class. It may be hard, but it's worth it."

As we worked with more clients with more points of view, and as the framework evolved to apply more broadly across more varied situations, not just training, we began to rethink this contribution in some important ways.

This shift, you will note, aligns with our values: We believe we cannot prescribe values and beliefs for others. We believe you, the reader, know best what will serve your needs and purposes.

- -

Try This: Identify Your Values and Beliefs

1. Find a conversation partner. Think of a time you felt fulfilled or proud.

    - Share what happened, then debrief it with them. Ask:
        - What did you hear me say?
        - What did you hear I care about?

2. Recall what you tell your clients/participants/colleagues.

    - What do you say you care about?
    - What promises do you make?

3. Track your time.

    - What do you prioritize?
    - What do you spend time on?
    - What energizes you?
    - What drains you?

Using these and other reflections, here are some values that one of our clients identified for their facilitators:

- The wisdom is in the room.
- Everyone has a voice and we're all better for it.
- Silence often equals value.
- I don't know.

- -

You may notice that these values often show up as phrases or philosophies rather than single words as values usually do. We find that comes from diving deeply into the context and stating the values in a way that is tied to that environment. If your values surface more traditionally as one word (usefulness, connection, respect), that works just as well.

Managing Conflicting Values

Part of what can make it a challenge to behave in alignment with one's values is that our values can conflict, not just with organizational values, but with each other. Exploring universal values and how they might align or not can help us understand common challenges.

A major tech client that we work with takes their values very seriously. Their new-hire orientation was built around their values for many years, and performance assessments explicitly measure against values. But that does not mean values conflicts do not arise. Two of their values are "Move fast" and "Focus on long-term impact." You can imagine how trying to serve these two at the same time might cause confusion. If we are developing a new product, do we get something to market as quickly as possible, or build something that will transcend what the competition is building? When assigning responsibilities, do we do what we are best at ourselves, or delegate and coach to develop future leaders?

Shalom H. Schwartz's work elucidates why we often find ourselves with conflicting values. His original work posited ten, later expanded to nineteen cross-cultural, universal values that fall into four categories.[18,19] The categories fall along two axes: a personal versus a social axis and a self-protection versus self-expansion axis. They include self-direction, stimulation, hedonism, achievement, power, security, conformity, tradition, benevolence, and universalism.

By examining these axes, let alone the individual values, we can recognize where conflict is inevitable. Self-expansion will often feel at odds with self-protection, for example. Self-direction and conformity are hard masters to serve simultaneously.

As a facilitator, then, we can anticipate having to make values choices in the moment. Do I serve my desire for security or benevolence when I notice bias or aggression? (In other words, do I step in and say something directly? Do I check in later? Do I let things go and discuss with the speaker later one-on-one?) How do I reconcile my client's preference for tradition with their request for a more out-of-the-box approach? The point is not that these values must be in conflict, but that tensions arise that make choosing a move more challenging than simply trying to serve one belief or value.

Understanding Others' Values

The dilemma of managing conflicting values gets exacerbated when we need to manage not just our own personal values, but those of the groups we are serving and the organizations within which we are working.

---

18 Schwartz, Shalom H. (2022, May 10) "Schwartz Theory of Basic Values."[Blog post] i2insights.com
19 Schwartz, S. H. (2012). An Overview of the Schwartz Theory of Basic Values. On-line Readings in Psychology and Culture, 2(1). https://doi.org/10.9707/2307-0919.1116

Our values spring not just from individual desires and preferences, but from our culture and environment. Therefore, our most fundamental values can remain hidden from our conscious awareness, like water to David Foster Wallace's proverbial fish. In Wallace's 2005 commencement speech at Kenyon College, he shared this oft-quoted parable:

There are these two young fish swimming along

And they happen to meet an older fish swimming the other way

Who nods at them and says

"Morning, boys. How's the water?"

And the two young fish swim on for a bit

And then eventually one of them looks over at the other and goes

"What the hell is water?"

Recognizing our specific cultural narratives and values can help us identify where we might anticipate values conflicts with others. If we can see the water we swim in, we can notice when it starts to get murky. In other words, when we become aware of the environment or circumstances that surround us, we can recognize any conflict or changes.

Florence Kluckhohn and Fred Strodtbeck, in their work on Values Orientation Theory,[20] originally posited these

---

20 Kluckhohn, Florence R., and Strodtbeck, Fred L. (1961) *Variations in Value Orientations*; Publisher: Row, Peterson, Evanston IL.

five areas of "basic concern" that are universal in all cultures, with various assumptions or preferences in each category determining unique cultural dynamics:

Human nature: Are we innately bad, good, or some combination?

Relationship to the natural world: Are human masters of nature, submissive to it, or in harmony with it?

Time: Is a culture oriented most toward the past, present, or future?

Activity: Is a life well-lived about being (simply living life without working about accomplishment or development), becoming (leaning into an unfolding process of development), or doing (working hard and achieving goals)?

Social relations: What should the relationship be between the larger society and the individual: hierarchical, individually focused, or something they called collateral, in which everyone has a specific role and decisions should be made by consensus?

As facilitators, we must recognize that values live not just in individuals separate from context and background. Whether when meeting between departments, entering a new organizational culture, or traveling to a different country, when conflict arises, understanding that it may not be just individual differences at play, but cultural norms and values, can help shed light on how to respond most effectively. Something that might at first glance seem just confusing or obstructionist, may, in fact, be a values conflict at a very deep level that neither party is aware of.

Step 2: Pinpoint Behaviors

Once we are aware of our fundamental values and beliefs, the next step is to hone in on what our values look like in action. How do they manifest when interacting with others and making your facilitative choices? If I say I value inclusion, for example, what can I do or say that will create an inclusive environment? What do I need to protect against or stop doing?

Behaviors should be observable; imagine things you could do or say that could be captured by a video camera.

If we're looking to create inclusive environments, for example, behaviors might include the following:

 Set group agreements for naming and taking accountability for the impact of statements and actions, not just people's intent.

 Build in formal opportunities for introductions, connection, and trust-building.

 Ensure everyone gets a chance to speak and equalize speaking time.

 Design the space with a round table(s) or movable chairs, to avoid supporting structural hierarchies.

Behaviors to avoid could include:

 Allowing the high-status participants to monopolize the conversation.

 Arguing with people's feelings, opinions, or interpretations.

 Creating activities that exclude participants with physical limitations.

Sometimes identifying appropriate behaviors is easy; other times, we need to check ourselves and get external feedback. Our intentions do not always align with our impact.

For example, Therese was coaching Jax, a sales manager, who used an excessive amount of self-deprecating humor when he led sales training. If he forgot to mention a detail, he would say, "I must have left my brain at home!" If someone asked what time to return from a break, he would reply, "Leave it to me to not remember that detail," and if someone made an insightful comment, he would follow it up with, "See, you are better at this than me!" With each self-directed put-down, his audience grew more uncomfortable.

When Therese pointed out that pattern of behavior to Jax, he didn't see a problem with it. Rather, he saw it as expressing humility — a core value to him. What Jax didn't realize was that his behavior wasn't in alignment with that value because people interpreted it as a lack of confidence and self-sabotage. Moreover, his disparaging remarks, directed inward, reflected a focus on himself and not others, which was the opposite of what he intended. When asked to describe what humility meant to him, he defined it as being modest, down to earth, approachable, and not arrogant. Therese worked with Jax to identify behaviors that better aligned with and reflected his value of humility; for instance, acknowledging when he learned something new, or giving examples of when he made a mistake and the lessons he learned.

Let's take another example from the stated values of one of our clients: "The wisdom is in the room." This phrase, articulated by the learning and development team at a tech company, expresses the belief that people come with expertise and insight that is valuable for their colleagues to hear. It rejects a model in which the facilitator shows up as the main expert, imparting all the knowledge to empty vessels. What behaviors might demonstrate this belief? The facilitator might:

 Ask lots of open-ended questions with no right or wrong answers,

 Ask participants to reflect on and share their experiences.

 Design opportunities for the participants to share best practices and peer-coach.

Alternatively, we would know that a facilitator did not truly hold this value if they:

 Spend most of the session lecturing.

 Ask closed "gotcha" questions with answers participants had to guess correctly.

Answer any questions the group posed themselves.

When they are written in black and white, we can easily recognize the values-based behaviors. But in action, we often slip out of alignment. Lofty principles can be hard to hang onto in practice.

To understand the relationship between values and behaviors, let's look at examples of the same expressed value in practice from some of Kat's company's clients. Three of them shared the stated belief that "Professional development is important, and should be prioritized." Their behaviors, though, differed significantly.

Example 1, an ad agency, was very hands-off in collaborating on the customization of the leadership program we were facilitating. We showed up on the day of delivery and began with our normal conversations about agreements. We asked the group to agree to put away their electronic devices until the breaks. (There is scary research about how distracting — even just having a cell phone out on the table — can be). For the first and only time we can remember, the participants said, "No."

"What?" we said.

"No," the participants repeated. "We have actual work to do and we can't be away from our teams for three whole hours."

"Oh," we replied. "We were under the impression that your managers cleared your schedules and backed you up. We designed this program with the understanding that that would allow you to focus."

"Nope," they said. "Our clients are king. We can't be away for this."

And they weren't. It was hard to get them to look up from their screens for any length of time, and no small-group work was possible without half the room simply turning to their regular work.

Example 2, a large tech company for which we also designed and launched a manager training program, easily agreed upfront to our suggestion to put away phones and laptops. But within the first hour or so of our two-day offsite, most had retrieved their electronic friends and were feeling pulled back into the gravitational force of their usual schedules. Unlike at the ad agency, however, the managers expressed frustration and remorse. They wanted to be present and focused, but didn't feel they were getting the organizational support they had been promised.

When we discussed the situation with the program sponsors, they doubled down on their commitment to prioritizing development. They arranged to send information to each participant's manager before the program soliciting their help in freeing up their reports' time.

"Treat course time as PTO," they said. Senior directors were engaged to open the sessions.

As a result, at the next workshop, participants found they were much more able to fully focus, and they reported that even their internal nagging voices interrupted less.

Example 3, at Client 3, an investment bank, our contact took us aside before we led our first session with their senior directors and said, "Look, I know you usually say something like, 'Let's maximize our time together by putting away our cellphones and closing our laptops so we can focus,' but these folks call on the president (meaning the President of the United States) and people like that, so they really can't put their phones away. We value what you're doing or we wouldn't have flown all these senior directors in, but there are priorities."

Although we took the warning to heart, the partners stayed very focused and committed during the session itself. They, more than anyone, valued their time and were not about to waste it on multitasking. If someone needed to take a call, they stepped outside and then returned, phone out of sight, and the workshop proceeded effectively.

Even though these three organizations stated the same value, what they demonstrated differed tremendously. Although Client 1 paid lip service to the value "Professional development is important, and should be prioritized," they clearly valued other tasks more actively. In subsequent conversations with the executive team, the leaders acknowledged that the organization did not have a learning culture as much as they might theoretically like to have one. Traditional advertising culture revolves around meeting the clients' needs in nearly pathologically immediate and complete ways. The most obvious value demonstrated in our courses was "Clients come first no matter what." And this seemed reasonable enough.

The challenge arose when that value interfered with the development and growth of the organization and the individuals in it. Eventually, this led to a reduction in client services, lower-quality work, and attrition. Finally, we, along with the Learning and Development team, realized that to behave in alignment with the professional development value, we would need to design learning opportunities that were even briefer and supported by asynchronous, just-in-time resources. There was no point in shaming people or pretending we were acting in alignment with our values. We had to ask, "How could we really do it."

What do these examples show us? It is one thing to profess values, quite another to identify, let alone live up to, the behaviors that embody them.

Bottom line: Once you have identified your beliefs and values, get clear on how you see those showing up for you in your context and then figure out what you can say and do to bring those values to life.

Koppett Company Values

Here are the identified values for Kat's company (Koppett) along with the accompanying behaviors. Whenever we facilitate, these behaviors are top of mind. The behaviors that feel most relevant in formal facilitation environments are in bold type.

WISDOM

We cultivate deep understanding and continuous learning. This includes drawing from past experience and engaging in ways that generate curiosity, humility, open-mindedness, perspective, empathy, discernment, and sound judgment.

1. We engage with each other and the world with curiosity.
2. We seek to learn from our experiences and interactions.
3. We respect complexity and invite the opportunities it brings.
4. We bring courage to act and serve what's needed.
5. We strive for excellence in our work.

PLAY

We delight in the small moments of laughter and fun, and we are committed to building collaborative joy together. This means we engage with levity and creativity, celebrating our wins and our failures as opportunities to connect, grow, and imagine new possibilities together.

1. We endeavor to get on the same wavelength and co-create adventure.
2. We schedule time for pure creative and joyful activities for their own sake.
3. We infuse fun into activities to create learning and growth opportunities.
4. We recognize and support different modes and styles of play.

CARE

Grounded in nourishment, kindness, and well-being, we act in ways that support mental-emotional-physical health, growth, and fulfillment. We actively tend to our internal culture, recognizing that by caring for ourselves, we are also best able to care for our clients and the larger communities in which we serve.

1. We ask for what we need.
2. We pay attention to what matters to others.
3. We practice appreciation and gratitude regularly.
4. We take good care of ourselves and each other.
5. We engage with kindness.

MEANING

Our work is guided by the aim to have a positive impact on others and the world around us — extending our capacity to bring about lasting change. We commit to co-creating meaning with our partners and clients, including creating services, experiences, and products that deliver on the goals and outcomes we promise.

1. We create a shared purpose with our colleagues and partners.
2. We work to catch and share the best stuff.
3. We nurture love, strength, and joy in service of a larger life purpose.
4. One size fits one — we design learning experiences that match the unique needs of others.
5. We say yes to colleagues and partners doing important social justice work.

ADAPTABILITY

We respond willingly to the demands of the moment even when they pull us away from our plans. We consciously and willingly flex to meet the needs of our widely diverse clients and partners. We relish the opportunity to be present.

1. We take risks even when the outcome is uncertain.
2. We change the agenda if that serves the goal better.
3. We accept and build with what exists.
4. We devote time and energy to stretching and growing together.
5. We demonstrate versatility.

Step 3: Walk the Talk

Of course, we all know that acting in alignment with our values in any circumstances is easier said than done. As mentioned at the beginning of this chapter, the simple act of consciously naming our values and the behaviors that demonstrate them will take us a long way toward walking our talk, but what happens when, as we have seen in some of these examples, the heat gets turned up or values conflict?

For example, we may believe that "the wisdom is in the room," but when we feel pressured for time, can we access the courage to ask open-ended questions, or do we default to spraying knowledge? The first option might be the behavior most aligned with our values — and even the soundest choice in terms of understanding and retention — but our desire for control or a feeling of certainty that we have checked all our boxes might steer us toward the second one.

Think about values around inclusion. How good are we at truly living in alignment with that professed value when we feel personally challenged? Let's say when a participant in a meeting tells us something we said or did offended them, or that they felt excluded. Are we open to the feedback, or do we get defensive and justify our choices? What if a person with power (perhaps our boss or the person who hired us) pushes for a certain kind of decision or process? How courageously do we make space for other opinions and voices then?

Acknowledging that we are not always walking our talk is the first step to figuring out how to shift to be more in alignment.

Let's take the relatively straightforward example earlier of the ad agency that said they valued "professional development" but actually defaulted to "the client always comes first." Upon reflection, their Learning and Development team recognized that the culture would not change very much in this regard, and continuing to battle to get folks into longer in-person training sessions would fail. This happened, of course, because the organization had a strong conflicting value that they were serving very nicely. They saw that their habitual ways of running training couldn't work, so they reduced the time and amount of the in-person events and built asynchronous and just-in-time structures to support learning in other ways.

Mapping our values against our habitual behaviors can help us figure out when we are in and out of alignment.

Try This: Map Values to Behaviors

- Choose a key value or belief.

- Brainstorm observable behaviors that demonstrate that value or belief.

- Brainstorm behaviors that might undermine or be in conflict with that value.

- Reflect on your habitual ways of being and use the following table to map where those behaviors are and are not aligned with those that support your value.

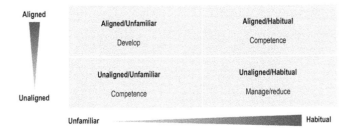

There's a reason we discuss Model Values and Beliefs as one of the first contributions. Your values should touch every choice you make, from where, when, and with whom you will meet to how you answer a question. And the facilitation excellence wheel embodies our facilitation values and beliefs. As you continue your journey to develop the rest of these mindsets and skills, keep identified values in mind and see how they inform what you do.

Chapter Takeaways

- Identify your core values and beliefs. They serve as a compass, guiding you toward choices that are reflected in your behaviors.

- Get curious about the values and beliefs of others, and how they may diverge from your own.

- Sometimes it's not just individual differences at play, but cultural norms and values of the group or the organization. Spotting those differences early can inform how to engage.

- Our intentions do not always align with our impact. How aligned are your values and beliefs with your behaviors? Ask for feedback.

4. Share Subject-Matter Knowledge

Displays expert knowledge and relates content
to audience priorities.

I possess relevant principles and knowledge.

I model relevant skills and abilities.

I scale my expertise to the needs and experience of others.

I hold my expertise with humility and am open to correction and addition.

In 2015, TV writer Will Stephen gave a TEDx Talk entitled "How to Sound Smart in Your TED Talk"[21] that, as of this writing, has garnered more than 12 million views. He starts off by stating that he has nothing to share, and true to his word, in hilarious fashion, he offers an entire meta TED Talk complete with all the stylistic tropes of the genre that was gaining widespread popularity at the time, but completely devoid of content.

"Hear that? That's nothing. Which is what I, as a speaker at today's conference, have for you all. I have nothing. Nada. Zip. Zilch. Zippo. Nothing smart. Nothing inspirational. Nothing even remotely researched at all. I have absolutely nothing to say whatsoever. And yet,

---

21 Stephen, William (2015, January 15). How to Sound Smart In Your TED Talk [Video]
YouTube https://youtu.be/8S0FDjFBj8o?si=xKuJJ98a8f4yc9PJ

through my manner of speaking, I will make it seem like I do," he begins. "I'm going to make a lot of hand gestures. I'm going to do this with my right hand. I'm going to do this with my left. I'm going to adjust my glasses. And then I'm going to ask you all a question. By a show of hands, how many of you all have been asked a question before? Okay, great, I'm seeing some hands. And again, I have nothing here," he continues.

Later in the talk, he shows graphs that include a pie chart showing that "the 'majority' far exceeds the 'minority'" and a bar graph labeled with just "influx," "outflux," and "agriculture."

Of course, the talk is not really devoid of content. Although Stephen may have only intended comic effect, he points to something profound: These behaviors and approaches proliferate because they work as tools to convey messages with impact. (Savvy readers may note some of the common tropes of the TED Talk genre that Stephen spoofs in the pages of this book.) But without actual substance at the heart of our communication, what is the point? The same tools and techniques, as Stephen demonstrates, can obscure legitimacy as much as support it, if no actual content gets served.

Subject-matter expertise is a double-edged sword. We can both over- and underestimate its importance. Having expertise does not make us skilled communicators. In fact, sometimes expertise can blind us to the needs of a group. Ask yourself: Have I ever relied too heavily on my expertise? Have I shown up with an enormous PowerPoint deck that prevented me from building rapport or engaging in a meaningful dialogue?

Of course you have! We all have. And the more knowledge or experience we have with a given topic or situation, the more likely we will make assumptions and over-index on giving advice, while squeezing out other voices and points of view. Expertise does not necessarily help you apply your knowledge and skill effectively in every situation.

Take Dr. Jameson, an expert in cancer research, who is often the smartest person in the room. When he addressed a room filled with peers, it was as if he spoke fluently in a distinct language only understood by fellow scientists. When his pharmaceutical start-up put him in front of investors, he stumbled. In that context, his depth of knowledge became a barrier to connecting because he was too focused on his content within his context, and he lacked the ability to shift the content he was sharing, let alone how he was sharing it.

On the other hand, if we lack enough relevant knowledge and skill, we can fail to understand important aspects of a given issue or dynamic. What do technical terms mean? What is the larger landscape of competitors and economic forces in a business discussion? What comments and concerns are most cogent and which are more about interpersonal dynamics? What skills, frameworks, tools, and approaches might be relevant and helpful? What kind of historical challenges and solutions exist in the space? All these are pieces of relevant knowledge useful to leaders in their roles.

In addition, the context in which we find ourselves having to communicate that expertise has a substantial impact on how much we need to know and what it will mean to effectively share it. The content we share in an eighteen-minute TED Talk, for example, will differ from the content we share in a sales call or team offsite meeting.

Because thinking about subject matter without context is like flying a plane without any navigation, the two Content contributions "Share Subject-Matter Knowledge" and "Suit the Context" are especially interdependent. Without a clear understanding of the audience, circumstances, or environment, we cannot know what subject matter to focus on in the first place. We recommend investigating these next two chapters together.

Developing the Message

"I have a thousand things swirling in my head that I could share with you," a client said in response to Therese's question. It was an exaggeration, of course, but the reality is there's never a lack of things to share when you're the subject-matter expert. The real challenge is figuring out what to share and what to leave out to avoid drowning people in a tidal wave of information that leaves them confused or overwhelmed.

We are often sought out to help leaders prepare to present during high-stakes moments: presenting a TEDx Talk, pitching a big idea to a board of directors, leading the orientation kickoff event for 500 new employees, or influencing a client to make a major investment. One of the most common mistakes we see among subject-matter experts is diving straight into creating PowerPoint slides when the starting point lies somewhere else entirely.

Instead of focusing on the answers, target what the audience wants and expects:

1. **Identify focus.** Clarify the key takeaway; consider your audience and what you want them to do differently.

2. **Clarify benefits and behaviors.** Step into the shoes of your audience and identify what's in it for them while balancing that perspective with the obstacles and challenges.

3. **Develop key content.** Get specific with what you need your audience to understand and do.

This is an iterative process because the more you reflect on these three steps, the more it informs your answers.

We've broken the steps down into a series of questions to help you identify and prioritize what to share. Let's take a closer look.

Identify Focus

 What's my key message?

 Who's my audience?

 What do I want them to do differently?

Consider these three questions as a set of interconnected ideas to reflect on in tandem and iteratively. The more you know your audience, the more it informs your key message and the more you distill your key point, the more laser-focused you become in defining what you want them to do differently.

What's My Key Message?

This might be obvious and simple, but it's often overlooked and not always easy: We know in our head what we mean, but the more we can distill the point — the moral of the story — into one key sentence, the more we start getting on track.

Kat participates each year as a speaker coach for a Chamber of Commerce Entrepreneurial Boot Camp, designed to develop burgeoning business owners. About three-quarters through the program, she helps the members of each cohort prepare for a "Shark Tank"-like competition in which they pitch their business concepts to a group of bankers and investors. The winner receives a cash prize and publicity as the boot camp winner.

In answer to the question about his key message, Adam, a bakery owner fresh from culinary school, started with, "Mass-produced grocery store bakery items are full of chemicals and additives, and I want to make it feasible for people to get made-from-scratch baked goods in their neighborhood that taste good and are good for you. Plus, I'll reinvest my income within the community by buying my raw ingredients like eggs, honey, and milk from local farmers. We haven't had a locally owned bakery in our town in over ten years, and it's time to change that."

Kat challenged him to distill it to one sentence his audience (the bankers and investors) would remember.

He thought further and reframed it as: "Adam's Bakery is filling an unmet need in the community for healthy baked goods." With this far more clear and memorable key message, he was ready to answer the next question.

Who Is My Audience?

When Therese's son was younger, they would play a game where she had to guess the song in his head and the only clues were his hand claps that synced to the beat of the song. The game originated from Chip and Dan Heath's book, *Made to Stick*.[22] Therese's son was always incredulous when she couldn't correctly identify simple, well-known songs like "Twinkle, Twinkle Little Star" or "Happy Birthday." Something similar happens all the time with presentations: We hear the music in our head but our audience only hears clapping and we're frustrated when they don't get it.

Ironically, the more expert we are, the more we can fall prey to misaligning how we talk about our topics and what our audience understands. Asking the question "Who is my audience?" leads to a more conscious adaptation of content (and style) to the needs of the specific listeners.

There's a YouTube show called "Levels"[23] where an expert is challenged with explaining complex concepts like black holes or machine learning to five people. The catch? They must tailor their explanation and make it

---

22 Heath, C., & Heath, D. (2007) Made to Stick: Why Some Ideas Survive and Others Die. Random House
23 WIRED; Levels channel [videos]YouTube; https://youtube.com/playlist?list=PLibNZv5Zd0dz-S1M_zimRtPCIQg6Fcd8x&si=qT8tJeW8QzRA8_9X

easily digestible to a five-year-old, thirteen-year-old, college student, graduate student, and peer in their field. By considering the context of the audience, they are able to effectively offer expertise in a way that resonates and that target audience can consume.

In Kat's story, she asked Adam what he knew about his audience and she spotted a problem: He was focused on the neighborhood residents — his intended customers. And while that's true in his bakery, his immediate audience was people who weren't "in the house": bankers and investors. They care about the business case, return on investment, and mitigating risk. They might never come to the bakery and sample its goods.

Adam quickly pivoted and said, "No problem! I've got the business case, capital equipment expenditures, and cash flow projected for the first twelve months, and — "

Kat replied, "That's great! It's naturally their first priority, but go one step deeper. What do you know about them? What might they individually care about?"

Through a quick online search, Adam discovered that one banker writes a blog about veganism while another sponsors several community 5k walk/run events along with mobile health screenings, all reflecting a value on health and fitness.

With this insight, Adam realized his key message needed to be refined because it wasn't considering his key audience enough, so he revised it:

Adam's Bakery is filling an unmet need in the community for healthy baked goods.

Adam's Bakery — Fueling the Local Economy and Community with Healthy Baked Delights

The answer to Who is my audience? can uncover more complexity than you might anticipate. Rarely does an audience consist of only one listener — even if there is only one person present. There are hidden audiences to consider. For instance, imagine a salesperson pitching a product to the head of IT who is eager to buy the latest software. Meanwhile, the VP of purchasing, not in the room but an influential decision-maker, is part of the larger but hidden audience. The IT leader is balancing her perspective with the purchasing colleague, who reminded her, "Vendors are taking advantage of us. We need better terms and a more generous payment plan." The salesperson needs to consider both priorities, values and opinions, not just the person looking back at them.

In our workshops, we demonstrate the importance of thinking deeper about your audience through an activity called the 500-Year Conversation. In pairs, person A is from the current day and person B takes on the persona of someone from 500 years ago (the 1500s), well before electricity, steam engines, and cars were invented. (Zippers weren't even invented for another 300 years.)

The goal is for person A to get their partner from 500 years ago to understand a current day object, like a microwave or contact lenses. It's trickier than you'd think. For instance, person A explaining how a microwave works describes pushing buttons to turn it on, while a confused person B imagines buttons on their shirt. Through laughter and a bunch of missteps, people learn how often we make assumptions about our audience and what they know and don't know. By thinking deeply about who your audience really is, you can put a laser focus on their knowledge values and desires instead of on your own.

What Do I Want My Audience to Do Differently?

This question keeps our attention on the audience and on the change we're trying to effect. While the first question, "What's my key message?," spotlights the core idea or takeaway, this question brings what needs to change to the surface.

When Kat coached Adam the baker on this question, his initial answer was, "Well, I want people to buy my baked goods."

It's a great answer when the primary audience is the general public, but he was in the middle of a competition with a different audience. Kat redirected him to think about the bankers and investors once more.

"Ah, right!" Adam replied. "I want them to believe in my business, trust that I'm a good business owner, and invest."

Kat smiled and nudged him to go one step further. "Yes! And then what do you want this audience to do differently?"

Adam replied, " I want the panel to award me the prize above my competitors. That's what I want them to do differently."

When you answer this question, push yourself to think of specific behaviors wherever possible. Don't limit your answer to feelings or knowledge alone.

We were helping a retail client, Cheryl, redesign her company's orientation day. As she showed us the forty-page deck featuring a run-through of more than 100 SKUs in women's dresses, we asked her why she was using that deck.

"They need to know this," was all she could manage at first.

"You know folks won't remember all this, right?"

"Yes, but I need to get through it."

We couldn't let that stand. "*Why?*" we asked. "What is it you want them to be able to *do* after orientation?" We reiterated that we were pretty sure her audience would not be able to recall or regurgitate all this information, so what was the point?

She replied, "We want them to feel like they are already starting to know our business on their first day."

We pressed a little further, asking again, "What do you want the new hires to do differently after they experience your orientation?"

She paused and said, "I want them to start assimilating into our culture. It's expected that people speak up and actively contribute in conversations, even if they aren't experts. People who stay silent and stick with the status quo have a hard time here. I guess what I really want is to get new hires operating that way immediately."

The actual behavior she wanted was new hires actively engaging by asking questions, sharing their understanding, and speaking up when they were confused. She had thought that meant they needed knowledge of all the products. But upon reflection, she realized there were skills and mindsets far beyond knowledge of the list of product codes that would be more helpful in the behavioral shift she desired.

With that clarity, our client rethought the entire design of the orientation. She explained what a SKU was, shared just a few examples, and then sent the participants on quests to discover things they didn't know about the company's products and processes. This built their comfort by embracing their curiosity and then grew their comfort and skill at finding information — the behaviors Cheryl actually wanted to instill.

Try This: Identify Focus

Your turn! Pick a specific situation and answer the following questions.

What's my key message? (Distill it to one sentence.)

Who is my audience? (What do they already know or don't know? What do they value?)

What do I want my audience to do differently? (Describe desired behaviors as much as possible.)

Clarify Benefits and Behaviors

You might be thinking, "Got it! *Now* can I get to prepping my slides?" Hold on. We may be clearer about our intention and what we want them to do. We may even have started to think about who our audience is. But we need to go deeper before we can truly know what information to share.

The next set of questions shifts the focus from "Why do I care?/What do I want" to "Why do *they* care and what are the obstacles?" These help hone the message, in a balanced way, with the audience in mind.

What's in It for Them?

Our baker, Adam, thought of it this way: "What's in it for the panel to give me the prize money and not my competitors?" He brainstormed his answers. What's in it for the bankers/investors is:

 My business plan, above others, offers a better return on investment, bringing more economic growth to the area, which the panel can advertise (and take some credit for).

 Baked goods are popular with all demographics and will bring the most press and free advertising to the accelerator program compared to competing projects.

 Choosing Adam is an easy, defendable choice compared to his competition (it isn't controversial).

Adam took a step back and noticed how distinctive those answers were for his audience versus what's in it for his customers or for him. He turned to Kat and said, "Now I get it! I'm ready to work on the slides now."

With a grin, she said, "Not so fast."

What Are the Obstacles and Challenges?

Identifying and addressing obstacles is just as important as highlighting the features. No matter how much someone values a solution, if the obstacles to implementation are too great, behavior won't change. You might not view something as a risk, but does your audience view it as a threat?

Addressing real or perceived obstacles proactively and acknowledging them instead of downplaying them signals that you are balanced and objective. In Adam's case, he knew the risks: In an economic downturn, consumers tighten their spending on non-essentials, like baked goods. Another risk was the fluctuating costs of goods — some of his competitors' businesses wouldn't be facing those headwinds.

Kat encouraged him to think a little deeper. She asked, "Adam, might the bankers and investors consider it risky that you've never run a business before?"

He replied, "I guess. I never thought of it that way."

Bringing all those potential challenges to the surface, while uncomfortable, allowed Adam to consider the countermeasures. In a downturn, he'd shift from higher-priced goods and redirect more resources to basic necessities like bread. He had market research to suggest that in an economic downturn, people turn to single-serving comfort baked goods, like cookies or cupcakes, even more. He'd hire a business coach to help ensure he was running the business in a fiscally responsible way.

Feeling equipped with a plan and data, he was eager and ready to address the potential obstacles. By confronting the challenges and obstacles, he was able to consider another factor: The bakery was more recession-proof than some the ideas of his competitors, which could be another success story for the Chamber of Commerce.

Try This: Clarify Benefits and Behaviors

• Continue reflecting on your project and ask yourself these questions to clarify benefits and behaviors.

• What's in it for them?

• What are the obstacles and challenges?

Develop Key Content

You might be itching to start on that PowerPoint slide deck, but there's one final question to answer. Then, we promise, you can craft those slides to your heart's content.

Now that you have gleaned clarity and depth about your intention and your audience, you are ready to identify what you need your audience to understand/feel/do. If you're thinking *Didn't I already do that when I identified the focus?* not quite. In this step, you're identifying what you need to impart to get your listeners from where they are to where you want them to be.

Or put another way, given my key message and the action I want my audience to take, how do I need to move them — intellectually and emotionally? What do they need to believe is possible? How do I need to shift their beliefs? What tools and paths do I need to provide?

What Do I Need My Audience to Understand/Feel/Do?

"Okay, Adam, what do you need the bankers and investors to understand, feel, or do?" asked Kat.

His eyes lit up as he replied, "I want them to name me the winner because they believe I've got the best business plan, and I'm the most capable entrepreneur."

Kat smiled, "Yes! And to do that, what else do they need to understand/feel/do?" This is where Kat enhances her role as facilitator by helping Adam make it more possible to have the impact and gain the results he seeks.

That got Adam thinking deeper. "Well, I don't think they'll just give me the award without vetting my qualifications, reviewing my business plan in depth, maybe even talking to a few of my references. And I definitely want them to experience the quality and value of my product by tasting it. Then they'll understand the soundness of my business plan and product quality validating my key point: Adam's

Bakery fuels the local economy and community with healthy baked delights."

With that question answered, Adam got to work on planning how he'd make it easier for the bankers and investors to take action. He planned to bring references, copies of the business plan for each audience member, and a basket of whole-grain muffins, including vegan and gluten-free options.

Remember to identify the content *most relevant* for the specific audience. Just because you know or believe something doesn't mean it is relevant to the group you are speaking to, or the objective of the conversation.

Types of Content

Finally, you are ready to identify the essential ingredients of the presentation. What will move our listeners from the current to the desired state? In asking this, we point ourselves toward three kinds of gaps to close. Each type requires us to take a different approach.

Knowledge: Knowledge is information that can be transferred and learned directly through written or spoken means. For example, you can bake a cake by reading a recipe on the back of a cake mix box. All you need to know is the number and amounts of ingredients (eggs, water, oil), the order of mixing dry and wet ingredients, and how long to bake it. Knowledge can vary in terms of level of complexity and require prerequisite knowledge or context to be understood, but for the most part, if the directions can be understood and retained (or referenced), it is usable. When thinking about what a listener needs to know, we think about this:

 What information should be included?

 At what level of complexity or detail should it be offered?

 What will maximize understanding and retention?

Skills: Skills are capabilities that are developed through practice. For example, for a chef preparing a Fugu puffer fish, the Fugu must be dismembered using special knives and then quickly separated into edible or poisonous parts to contain the neurotoxin, exponentially more deadly than cyanide. (Only licensed chefs in Japan are allowed to serve Fugu.) Skill-building, by definition, usually takes behavioral effort and repetition.

In presentations, we cannot always build the skills of our audience — that happens over time. In training situations, conversely, teaching and exercising new skills can and should be the goal. When we don't distinguish knowledge transfer from skill development, we can end up spraying information that does not really shift anything behaviorally, and overpredicting results. To shift what people are able to do, we ask this:

 What tools and materials are necessary to support development?

 What opportunities for experiential practice can I provide?

 What feedback and coaching can be offered?

Attitudes/beliefs: We spent a fair amount of time on defining beliefs in our "Model Values and Beliefs" and "Managing Yourself" chapters. Our mindsets and stories we tell ourselves regarding a given topic can support understanding and the commitment to developing skills, or they can undermine behavior, even if knowledge and skills are present.

For example, saying "I am a good cook." If someone already believes they are a good cook, that could motivate them to engage more seriously in a culinary arts course, seek new techniques, and practice new skills. On the other hand, the same belief might spark resistance to new learning, if the participant feels disrespected or talked down to. Conversely, someone who believes "I'm a terrible cook" might not be able to engage in development until they shift their self-talk and ambient narratives about what it takes to be capable.

An attitude or belief may or may not be aligned with an objective assessment of one's skills. Kat's four-year-old daughter, for example, developed a strong belief in herself as an excellent cook and decided she could make carrot soup on her own. Refusing any help or input, she put a bowl of water and baby carrots in the microwave. Although that first experiment didn't turn out the way she expected, her confident mindset motivated her to learn about cooking and eventually develop actual culinary skills.

Try This: Develop Key Content

What do I need my audience to understand/feel/do?
(Identify the specific knowledge, skills, and belief gaps
you want to close.)

Intellectual Humility

In addition to being aware of what we do know
(remember that curse of knowledge), to be effective
presenters, teachers, and guiders of groups, we must pay
attention to what we don't. Bill Gates reads fifty books a
year.[24] Albert Einstein is attributed as saying, "I have no
special talents. I am only passionately curious." Warren
Buffett estimates he spends 80 percent of his working
day reading and thinking.[25] Physicist Brian Cox said, "In
science, there are no universal truths, just views of the
world that have yet to be shown to be false."[26]

A common trait among many world-renowned experts
is a willingness to acknowledge what they don't know, to
stay open to the possibility that the facts might change
as more knowledge is gained. It's like a mental safeguard
against the belief that "I have all the answers." Intellectual
humility is the ability for people to realize their potential
fallibility when developing their attitudes and beliefs.[27]

24 "Did You Know Bill Gates Reads 50 Books a Year?"(2022, May 20) Penguin Books Blog Australia

25 Winfield, C. (2015, July 28)"This is Warren Buffett's Best Investment Advice" Time. com https://time.com/3968806/warren-buffett-investment-advice/.

26 BMAT Worked Solutions. (n.d.). 2019 Section 3 Question 2. https://bmatworkedsolutions.wordpress.com/2019-section-3-question-2/.

27 Zmigrod, L., Zmigrod, S., Rentfrow, P. J., and Robbins, T. W. (2019). The psychological roots of intellectual humility: The role of intelligence and cognitive flexibility. *Personality and Individual Differences* 141, 200–208. https://doi.org/10.1016/j. paid.2019.01.016.

We all know someone who thinks they know everything. The know-it-alls in our lives are quick to offer their opinion, often without listening to other perspectives, and can be a major hindrance to progress and innovation. We appreciate subject-matter experts who are learn-it-alls — open to new ideas, curious about the unknown, and willing to learn from their mistakes. Knowledge is never static.

In a 2018 Pepperdine[28] study of intellectual humility, the researchers stated, "Knowing (and being willing to admit) what you don't know may be the first step to seeking new knowledge." In a similar study by social psychologists at Duke University,[29] the findings were that the intellectually curious do better at evaluating evidence and were more effective at discerning quality, fact-based arguments from weaker ones.

Approaching conversation with curiosity and openness, even when we are the identified experts in the room, enables us to connect more deeply with our audiences and continually grow our own knowledge, skills, and mindsets so we can be of further service to our conversational and learning partners.

Conveying the Message

We started this chapter by reminding ourselves that content (the what) matters separately from our process

28 Elizabeth J. Krumrei-Mancuso, Megan C. Haggard, Jordan P. LaBouff & Wade C. Rowatt (2020) Links between intellectual humility and acquiring knowledge, *Journal of Positive Psychology* 15:2, 155-170, DOI: 10.1080/17439760.2019.1579359.
29 Leary, M. R., Diebels, K. J., Davisson, E. K., Jongman-Sereno, K. P., Isherwood, J. C., Raimi, K. T., Deffler, S. A., and Hoyle, R. H. (2017). Cognitive and Interpersonal Features of Intellectual Humility. Personality and Social Psychology Bulletin 43(6), 793–813. https://doi.org/10.1177/0146167217697695.

(the how). Communication theorist Marshall McLuhan reminds us that "the medium is the message"[30] and although we have artificially deconstructed our contributions as if they are distinct and stand alone, in fact, we cannot totally separate the what of our subject matter from the how that information is delivered.

How a message is communicated shapes the message itself and influences how it is perceived by the audience. Television, for example, demands a different kind of visual excitement than a newspaper does, and this has impacted how news stories are chosen and reported, and the impact they have on the receiver. Breaking up with someone over text — even if the words are the same — does not have the same impact as having a conversation in person.

When it comes to deciding on the best medium for delivering your message in a persuasive way, think beyond your habitual ways of communicating to consider the impact you want to have and the preferences of your audience. Your parents might access information by reading the newspaper while you prefer a TikTok or YouTube video. Even with in-person conversations, you have many choices about the kinds of visuals, materials, and styles of communication that best suit your context.

We work with a lot of clients who fall into the pattern of thinking that PowerPoint is the only medium for delivering content. And while that might be expected, we think it's a missed opportunity to break from the norm and stand out among a sea of experts.

---

30 McLuhan, M., and Lapham, L.H. (1994) Understanding Media: The Extension of Man. MIT Press.

Imagine a Lean Six Sigma expert, Shamina, offering process improvement recommendations about the patient intake process to hospital administrators. She starts by delivering a PowerPoint detailing how her proposal will address the problem. She notices some yawning and a few people fighting to keep their eyes open. She pauses and says, "I'll give you an example." She describes fourteen-year-old Connor, who has muscular dystrophy and averages three trips a year to their ER, and explains how the improved process would make his life easier. Her audience perked up and clearly paid attention.

By pivoting away from the PowerPoint, she regains her listeners' attention. By connecting the information to a human being, Shamina facilitates empathy, engagement, and interest in her audience, and increases the likelihood that they would support her ideas.

This stokes questions about feasibility. Now, Shamina has another choice. She can revert to presenting details and facts, or pivot to a more interactive way of answering the questions by demonstrating how the intake process could work. She thinks, *The fastest way to help them understand is to show them*, so she does a mini role-play from the patient's perspective.

Once her audience experiences how the process might work, they are motivated to go deeper, so our expert returns to the presentation. At the end of the meeting, the hospital administrators are more ready to move forward and our expert offers to use the next meeting to teach them how to manage through change, knowing a big obstacle will be to get the ER coordinators on board with the transition.

You are an expert among experts when you know how to activate your subject-matter knowledge based on your audience's reaction. If you're looking for more about how to present, visit the Establish Presence chapter next and Engage with Story in the chapter after that. We'll help you expand your choices on content delivery methods. While not exhaustive, we'll dive into two options for persuading audiences — analogy and metaphor.

Analogy and metaphor are ways to explain and communicate complex or abstract ideas in a more relatable way. According to a study in the *Journal of Consumer Research*,[31] analogies are engaging and convincing because they provide a familiar reference point for your audience. By tapping into your audience's existing knowledge and experiences, you help them connect with your message in a more meaningful way.

Analogies and metaphors, by comparing things that are familiar to situations more novel, deepen understanding and retention. Analogies and metaphors can be simple images that become touch-stone references, or full-fledged conceptual frameworks to help guide understanding and approach. For example, starting a new business is like planting a seed in a garden. Just as a gardener must be patient and persistent to see the fruits of their labor, a business owner must put time and effort into seeing their business succeeds.

Stephen Covey's metaphor of "big rocks first,"[32] for example, has become part of the zeitgeist when speaking

31 Campbell, M. C., Warren, C., and Prokopec, S. (2016). An Analogy-processing Perspective on Communication and Persuasion. *Journal of Consumer Research* 43(4), 555–573.
32 Covey, S. R. (1989). The 7 Habits of Highly Effective People. Free Press.

about prioritization, even when many people don't know the whole narrative of where it came from. (Covey's image is trying to fit big rocks, small pebbles, and sand into a jar. When you put the big rocks in first, the smaller bits will flow around them and fit. But if you start by putting sand and pebbles in the jar, there won't be a way to fit in the big rocks.)

Try This: Create a Metaphor

Start with your main point. (We need to create market awareness about our new service.)

Think of more descriptors. (We want to get attention, prompt action, generate excitement, amplify the message.)

Then, think of things in common with those descriptors. (We could use a bullhorn, microphone, viral meme, town crier.)

Find a comparison. (We need everyone to shout from the rooftops about this new initiative.)

Demonstrate: Show vs. Tell

One way to think about shifting your medium is to do the behavior you are advocating for, rather than simply talking about its value. We are big fans of putting your money where your mouth is. It can be more credible, compelling, and convincing to demonstrate or show something versus explain it through words.

Therese was working with the chief marketing officer of a medical start-up who wanted leadership training for their VPs and directors. When she mentioned the skill of listening, the CEO said, "No, we don't need training on that. Our leaders have to listen all day."

She felt her words, explaining the value of advanced listening, were failing her, so she asked if she could do a little demonstration of what she meant. They obliged and the chief marketing officer agreed to play along. She invited him to start describing a business challenge. As he spoke, she restated the essence of his issue. Then she asked him to stop and repeat his challenge. This time, instead of listening, she gave him advice and asked questions that took him off track. It was a eureka moment! The CEO interjected and said, "Oh, my gosh. I see it now. That's our problem! We jump to problem-solving too quickly instead of really listening."

Demonstrating is a living, three-dimensional example. It brings concepts to life — like how a value looks in practice, how to do a task, how a technical skill or technique looks or sounds in action. When people can see it in action, they are more likely to understand and be persuaded.

Demonstrations don't need to take a lot of time. In Therese's example, the entire demonstration was under five minutes. The best places for demonstrations are when your verbal explanation isn't landing effectively or before you want people to try something for themselves.

Stay in Plain Sight

Make it easy to observe what you're trying to show. To demonstrate how to negotiate, you might use a visual that shows the steps or even state the step out loud throughout the demonstration (for example, "Watch me draw out their perspective first.").

Complex scenarios confuse the audience and can distract from what you're trying to highlight. A good rule of thumb is to offer only the context needed for people to imagine themselves in a similar situation. Like a good story, the audience will fill in the blanks themselves — and often be more engaged for not having to remember too much.

Be Relevant and Realistic

Make sure the situation matches people's reality. Otherwise, it's easy for people to dismiss the scenario as too scripted or "too perfect." As much as possible, use language that people would use in real life.

Try This: Show and Tell

Identify an upcoming situation where demonstrating or helping others experience your knowledge would lead to a better outcome; for example, more awareness, more understanding, more motivation.

Chapter Takeaways

- Before diving into slides, focus on understanding your audience's expectations and needs to shape your message based on what they want and expect.

- Continuously refine your content. Ask yourself:

  - **What's my key message?** (Distill it to one sentence.)

  - **Who is my audience?** (What do they already know or don't know? What do they value?)

  - **What do I want my audience to do differently?** (Describe behaviors as much as possible.)

- Anticipate and acknowledge both real and perceived obstacles to demonstrate a balanced and objective perspective. Consider:

  - **What's in it for them?**

  - **What's the obstacles or challenges?**

- Ask yourself: **What do I need my audience to understand/feel/do?** (Identify the specific knowledge, skills, and beliefs gaps you want to close.)

- When you want to persuade, look beyond your usual methods and consider your audience's preferences. Adapt your approach for maximum effectiveness.

5 Suit the Context

Demonstrate an understanding of group history, norms, and culture.

I gather relevant information about the history, experiences, and values of those I will engage with.

When interacting, I can speak about the group's dynamics, history, and culture accurately.

I notice and understand specific group dynamics.

I honor others' experience and needs by tailoring how I relate my expertise.

You are walking down the street. Behind you, you hear someone gruffly yell, "GET OUT OF THE WAY!" You watch them run across the street before the light turns red as you think, "What a jerk!"

Another day, someone else yells at you the same way, but they do so about debris falling from a third-story window that was about to land on your head. Now you're thinking, "What a hero!"

Context shifts meaning. It helps shape our understanding and our choices. Digital marketing and social media expert Gary Vaynerchuk said, "If content is king, then context is God."

Yale psychologist Robert Sternberg (1985) first popularized the term *contextual intelligence*, which says that a person's ability to react and adapt in any situation along with their creativity are equally important when evaluating a person's intelligence.

At this very moment, you are doing more work than you may realize. Your brain is applying context to what you're reading. You are making your own associations and connections to make meaning and realizing that the same words have different meanings for different people. If you are a new university graduate, a nurse practitioner, a school board member, a small-business owner, or a professor, you are applying your own experiences and stories to this book.

Early in Therese's career, she learned the value of context the hard way. She was deployed on a project in Europe, representing a U.S. corporate headquarters. She spent days preparing for a big meeting, ensuring she knew the content backward and forward, and could answer any questions about the project. She felt confident — until the first day, when she stared across the room at crossed arms, furrowed eyebrows, and a general resistance to anything she said. She was missing context.

She wasn't aware that European leaders had a general distrust of new initiatives from "corporate" because they came with a one-size-fits-all approach. Historically, their solutions didn't take into consideration the different culture, circumstances, and business dynamics outside the U.S. It didn't matter how solid or well-designed the content was. It didn't matter that Therese had years of experience and a master's degree. Because she didn't suit the context, the initiative, while successful in the U.S., struggled to succeed in Europe.

"We're unique." That's most people's perception about themselves or their organizations. And it's true. Every group operates in an environment that's uniquely theirs — the people, the challenge, the culture, the history, the goal. It's the facilitator's job to understand context, speak the "language," and create a tailored experience. Sometimes, especially when we have lots of experience, we can dismiss this reality.

Kat recalls how she learned not to be so quick to reject her clients' insistence on their uniqueness. For many years, she would joke that every time she met with a client who had hired her for her specialty in applied improvisation, at some point, they would say some version of the same thing: "We really believe what you do is of value, and we trust you, but these folks are different — they are _____ (doctors, academics, C-suite executives, administrators, etc.)." No matter what the group, Kat would laugh, they all expressed the concern that we would not effectively adjust our content and process to fit their specific needs and style. How silly, she would say. What clear proof that they are *not* different from others, raising the same concern. Why don't they trust us, she would think.

Then late one night, Kat was talking to a close friend and mentor who was to offer a workshop about facilitation to her colleagues at the Applied Improvisation Network the next morning. "I know you're an expert on this topic," she found herself saying. "But these folks are different; they're improvisers!" Almost immediately she realized what was happening. As the client, rather than the consultant, she could see all the specific nuances of her community: their strengths, weaknesses, preferences, and resistances. Never again would she dismiss a client's articulation of their individuality or see it as mistrust.

Beyond professional identity, industry trends, regulations, and hot topics can differ not only from business to business but moment to moment. Unconscious bias, behaviors, jargon, and habits can be subtle and difficult to read and interpret if you are the "outsider." Some voices may dominate and drown out others. Some messages may only be communicated between the lines. Scars might be hard to see and run deep, making it difficult to gather complete and authentic information for all sources.

A leader's awareness of context might be even more important than explicit subject-matter knowledge. As a guide who is working to manage focus and purpose, our awareness of unspoken dynamics, histories, and pressures can and should influence the choices we make as we employ all the contributions. What feels risky or safe in this environment? What values are paramount? What relationships are new; which are trusting and positive already; which need repair?

When we work with clients, we work hard to understand context. The map is not the terrain — that is, even a solid approach or methodology has to be aligned with the culture and dynamics. As we grow our context competency, we tailor what subject-matter knowledge we employ and how to deliver it so that it resonates with our audience.

Those who work internally and find themselves facilitating their peers and colleagues have both an advantage and traps to beware of. On the plus side, internal folks may have a deeper, more innate sense of the culture, style, and background of their community than facilitators who come from the outside. On the other hand, participants in a system can be blind to some realities, behaving like David Foster Wallace's image of fish who don't know what water is, since it is all around them. Consciously identifying contextual cues and adapting to them requires a deliberate kind of meta-awareness that can easily be skipped over.

For the first few years that we designed training for a global tech company, we could not facilitate the courses ourselves. Leadership believed strongly that it was unique and different, and that only internal employees would have the requisite awareness of context to appear legitimate and trustworthy by the participants in those courses. As the company grew, the ban on external facilitation lifted, but extensive training was required even for folks with substantial experience elsewhere. Many styles and approaches that might work in other places simply failed in this context. For instance, managers *support* their people in that company. A trainer who used words like *supervise* or *direct report* would immediately lose credibility. And whereas typically sharing experiences with other organizations might raise a trainer's status, at this tech company, those examples would often be met with dismissal as irrelevant.

It felt extremely important for the learning to feel warm, inclusive, and grounded. But even more importantly, it had to be high fidelity. Even the most well-respected external vendors had to highly customize their examples and flows. Some of the best facilitators we knew just didn't click in this environment. Others who were less experienced holistically thrived because they were able to absorb the specific style that spoke to the group.

Elements of Context

What should we look for specifically when we attempt to get a handle on context? Anything that influences people's attitudes and behavior counts, including culture, physical and professional environment, industry standards and norms, specific timing, individual personalities, and organizational or team history.

All of these contextual qualities intersect, and no one of them necessarily trumps another. Successful connection depends on identifying the most salient differences between your habitual ways of explaining or interacting and bridging those gaps. We get in trouble when we fail to notice contextual clues that might be out of alignment with our assumptions.

National culture is one example that can get either too little or too much attention. We pay too little attention when we assume that our brand of interaction and social norms are universal. Erin Meyer's culture map[33] identifies various scales of cultural difference and plots comparisons. Her scales include:

Communicating (Low-High context)

Evaluating (Direct-Indirect negative feedback)

33 Meyer, Erin (2014). The Culture Map. Hachette Book Press.

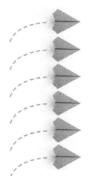 Persuading (Principles-Application first)

Leading (Egalitarian-Hierarchical)

Deciding (Consensual-Top-down)

Trusting (Trust-Relationship based)

Disagreeing (More-Less confrontational)

Scheduling (Linear-Flexible time)

To get a detailed sense of these scales, check out Meyer's book, "The Culture Map", provides a robust look at each of these scales. But even without a deep understanding of each, it can help to remember that what any of us might consider "normal" may, in fact, lie on the far end of a spectrum. The U.S., for example, in terms of persuasion, leans way to the right on the "application" end of the "Principles-Application first" scale. What might feel like practical, action-based, useful communication might be met with mistrust by those who want to know more about the process and data underlying conclusions.

Meyer tells the story of a presentation she gave in Japan that sparked her interest in these cultural differences. She gave a short presentation and then asked if there were any questions. No one said anything, so she sat down. After the event, her Japanese colleagues mentioned that he thought there had been questions. "But no one said anything!" Meyer responded. "But their eyes were bright," said her colleague.[34]

As facilitators, it behooves us to recognize that different groups may interact with us in different ways. Cultural

34 Meyer, E (2014) Business Speaker Erin Meyer: How Cultural Differences Affect Business. YouTube
Lavin Agency Speakers Bureau. https://youtu.be/zQvqDv4vbEg?si=xhqB4XUrwMM0-led

literacy is just one more area where we can expand our awareness and range.

That said, we pay too much when we attribute universal characteristics to a person or group based on nationality and imagine that they override other differences. Sivasailam (Thiagi) Thiagarajan, the guru of interactive design for learning, likes to say that there are often more differences between generations in one country than between cross-national members of the same generation.

Gather Insight

The bottom line is to pay attention to and investigate what might be unique and different in an environment. Here are some questions that can help you uncover and understand your context.

Context-Gathering Questions	
Culture	What adjectives describe the attitudes and norms? What are the shared values and how are they exhibited? What acronyms or a turn of phrase should we know? How formal or informal is the culture? What are the unwritten rules and general assumptions? What are the power dynamics? What adjectives describe the attitudes and norms?
Goals and Priorities	What is the group trying to achieve? What are the key priorities? How do decisions get made?
Industry	What are the biggest challenges facing this industry? How is this industry different from others? Who is a thought leader in this industry?
Timing	What is happening that might impact timing? When are major events or milestones that are important?
People	What roles and people hold the most power (formal or informal)? What is the dynamic among team members? How is success measured? What do you want me to know about you/your group?
History	What has happened in the past that might affect what we're doing now?

Context Clues

Sometimes what people share about the context is consciously or unconsciously skewed. In addition to asking direct questions, research and investigation can reveal context clues.

LinkedIn/social media: Search for commonalities, like schooling, hobbies, previous employers, or colleagues in common. Social media channels are a continuous way to stay in sync with what the client thinks and cares about.

Annual reports: For publicly held companies, learn about the state of the business, their mission, and vision.

Company websites: This might be an obvious place to look, but dig beyond the landing page. Read the bios of the executive team. Look at the open jobs and how the company positions itself to candidates.

Press releases: Staying up to date is important. Setting alerts for your clients can help external facilitators especially. An hour before Therese had a call with a client, for example, she received an automated alert that the company just announced an acquisition. With that fresh context, she changed her approach as the call started. Instead of jumping right into tasks, she spent time checking in with how the shell-shocked project leader was processing the news. Without that context, Therese would have missed a moment to show up as informed and empathetic.

The deeper and more nuanced your understanding of context, the more you can make effective choices about all the other contributions. By sharing your subject-matter expertise in the most appropriate and meaningful way, you can maximize your value to the group.

Chapter Takeaways

- A nuanced understanding of context enables you to make more effective choices.

- Be careful not to assume that your individual norms are universal.

- Contextual areas to pay attention to include Culture, Goals and Priorities, Industry, Timing, People, and History

- Look for clues and ask questions to deepen your contextual awareness.

6 Establish Presence

Confidently hold the space with credibility, patience, humility, and authenticity.

I can use my body, voice, and words intentionally to give and take focus.

I understand the language of status and power dynamics.

I recognize my habitual behaviors and "power comfort zone."

I am able to adapt my behavior to claim or offer attention and respect.

In her early twenties, Kat was part of a small theater company in New York, the Manhattan Stage Company, which included more than its fair share of highly talented, wicked-smart, and mostly very nice actors and playwrights. The company mounted everything from Shakespeare plays to original works, and she still thinks back on those folks as some of the most impressive she ever worked with.

Among them was a young actor and writer named Aaron Sorkin. Of course, these days, Sorkin is a recognized Oscar-winning screenwriter, playwright, and director. Back then, he was just one of a bunch of guys sharing an apartment in midtown Manhattan, tending bar at one of the Broadway theaters. Or was he? Somehow, even before he was *that* Aaron Sorkin, Aaron was Aaron. As soon as he walked into a room, the action revolved around him. No one who knew him then has expressed any surprise at his meteoric success.

Perhaps you have also had an experience with someone who seemed to exude animal magnetism strong enough to physically stop you in your tracks. This kind of personal presence has tremendous power. We are drawn to those who engage with presence. We trust those who project confidence and credibility. At a core level, we cede control and follow people, regardless of their formal rank or position who exude this personal charisma.

Presence of this sort is distinct from formal authority or subject-matter expertise. While both of those are commonly recognized sources of power in the workplace, the kind of presence we are discussing here is a more personal behavioral kind of power, and it is so fundamental to the human condition that we can often overlook its impact. When we do consciously tune into the core behaviors and mindsets of presence, we can exponentially increase our ability to connect, build trust, and influence others. This — our ability to learn to control and shift this type of power dynamically, in the moment — is what is so uniquely useful to concentrate on as a facilitation lever.

But wait, you may be saying. Isn't this kind of charisma an innate quality or talent that we cannot develop — something that is either built in or not? Something like height, that we have or simply don't? Typically, that is how such as ability is talked about. But we believe that much more can be taught than people assume. Just as great athletes or dancers may have innate abilities but train hard for years to realize their potential, so can any of us exercise our presence "muscles" and increase our personal power and influence to be ever more effective facilitators.

In the introduction to her book *The Second Circle*,[35] voice teacher and coach to actors, movie stars, leaders, and lay people Patsy Rodenburg relates how she came to challenge this orthodoxy. As a young teacher, already having worked with a wide variety of students and actors, some whom she found compelling and others who — even if beautiful or technically adept — left her cold, she asked her colleagues what they thought made the difference. "Some folks just have *it*," she was told. But this seemed not only an abdication of her duty as a teacher, but also a fundamentally unjust way of thinking. "I wasn't going to accept the inequality of human presence," she writes.

That commitment led her to develop a body of work that belies the assumption that presence cannot be developed. As she says, "You may not have the makeup, clothes, and lighting effects that enhance the stars, but you can still learn to find your own full charisma. All it is is energy. Present energy — clear, whole, attentive energy."

This means that *being present* is a strong component of *having presence*. The topics we discuss in the "Manage Yourself" and "Listen" chapters go a long way to strengthening your confidence and awareness and therefore your charisma. In this chapter, we want to unpack another element or awareness that can help you command attention, engage others, and establish credibility: status behaviors.

35 Patsy Rodenberg (2008). *The Second Circle.* W.W. Norton & Company, NY, pp. vi–viii.

Status

When we use the word *status*, people often think of the symbols of social status like money, or titles or fancy cars. But underneath all those symbols of status are a set of fundamental behaviors that signal either dominance or submission. Keith Johnstone, a theater director and innovator, recognized that status can be understood not as something we *are*, but as something we *do*. His work invites us to recognize how actively we confer or accept status through this behavioral language. Those interactions, then, not just titles or formal authority, determine who is perceived as holding power.

Psychologists John M. Levine and J. Keith Moreland say, "Humans, like other animals, usually have little difficulty reading signs of status and recognizing who defers to whom."[36] People high in status in a group tend to talk more and are freer to interrupt. They also display their status nonverbally, by standing erect, maintaining eye contact longer, and generally displaying signs of confidence.

Johnstone adds that high-status individuals tend to move fluidly and hold their heads still. Low-status behaviors, he says, include making themselves seem small physically and vocally; saying "um" and "uh" a lot; touching their face and hair; and trying to make eye contact, but looking away quickly. The first set of behaviors signals calm and security; the second indicates nervousness and a desire to please.

---

36 Levine, J. M., and Moreland, R. L. (1994). "Group Socialization: Theory and Research." *European Review of Social Psychology*, 5(1), 305–336. https://doi.org/10.1080/14792779543000093.

To reiterate, these behaviors may or may not be aligned with our formal rank or position. A high-ranking official may have personally low status or vice versa. Rowan Atkinson's "Blackadder" TV series, for example, built its entire comedy scaffolding on mismatches between official rank and personal status — a king behaving with low status, a servant with high-status behaviors. But this is the point: The comedy came from subverting our expectations. As human animals, we innately look to decipher status signals to figure out where we stand, so we know our (literal and figurative) place. (Don't worry, we are not advocating a predetermined caste system: quite the opposite. We are simply saying, we look to avoid status battles by trying to read the room. And we know how to do it.)

Although humans are great at reading these signals, most of us display and react to them habitually and unconsciously. These signs of dominance and submission affect nearly all our interactions, and yet very few of us pay attention to what we are signaling and responding to by actively noting that some kind of status dance is occurring. Moving our awareness of these dynamics and choices from passive to active allows us to diagnose and affect all sorts of interpersonal situations. (This is where we break out of pre-set roles and restrictions.)

Strengthening presence begins with this increased awareness of the physical and vocal moves that demonstrate different status levels. Becoming consciously aware of status dynamics is rather like swallowing Neo's red pill in "The Matrix" — although ideally not quite as depressing. All of a sudden, you can recognize the secret patterns behind our everyday realities.

At some point, nearly any presentation skills courses you have ever taken offer tips about how to stand or what to do with your hands. The specifics may differ — some courses will tell you to use your hands less, some more; some will tell you to stand still, some to pace — but what they are all designed to do, whether they know it or not, is teach you to take status. Look at some of the language some popular courses employ: "own the room," "command focus." Claiming high status is not always the goal, but when presenting, a high-status performance can often serve you well by attracting the attention of your audience and establishing credibility so your audience feels comfortable following you.

Claiming Status

When we are at the front of the room, presenting formally or guiding a conversation, we often want to claim focus by establishing high status. Note that the principles in play to demonstrate high or low status remain the same whether you are establishing presence in person or virtually, although some of the logistics may be different. Think of presence in person versus virtually as being on stage versus being on camera.

Center your body. To claim status, center your body and breathe deeply. Our friend Dion Flynn, a writer on "The Tonight Show" (and the actor who plays many roles in their sketches including President Obama), says that he spent tens of thousands of dollars and years in acting conservatory to learn two simple lessons: Relax your shoulders and breathe. Finding a neutral position that both looks and feels relaxed and grounded will allow you to start from a place of presence, command attention, and establish credibility.

Move with intention. In person, remember to move deliberately. Choosing a couple of specific spots in the room to move to and then maintaining stillness in-between intentional trips to those locations will help you avoid shuffling and shifting your weight in ways that undermine your authority and focus.

Gesture with clarity. Gestures, when employed effectively, aid communication tremendously. A study from the University of Chicago found that students learn significantly better when their teachers gesture, so gesturing does not just command attention but actually makes us better communicators. Why do some presentation skills programs caution against gesturing?

We can think of gestures in two categories: illustrative and self-soothing. The self-soothing gestures — touching our face and hair, adjusting our clothing, wringing our hands — lower your status and attract the ire of the presentation skills coach. Illustrative gestures — the ones that help explain, emphasize a point, and underscore meaning — are invaluable.

When gesturing in this fashion, do not be shy. In person, fill the space: Extend your arms fully. Allow your gestures to be higher than you might habitually place them. Where would you like folks to focus? Your face, right? If you gesture above your shoulders, you will be directing people to look there, rather than gesturing lower down and pointing them to less relevant areas.

Connect through eye contact. Perhaps the most powerful status indicator of all is eye contact, and using it well matters a great deal when it comes to presence. But sometimes when we start to think consciously about our use of eye contact, the whole issue just gets confusing and weird. Making unnatural eye contact can do more harm than good and create discomfort all around. Eye contact is also the skill that is the most different in person versus virtually.

In person, rather than thinking about making eye contact, we suggest working to *receive* eye contact. Look from person to person with the silent question, "Are you with me?" "Does that resonate?" "Are you getting this?" "How does that sound?" The point of eye contact in the context of presenting is to connect and build influence, not to dominate in some competitive fashion. We want to draw our audience in. Thinking about getting eye contact from our listeners rather than delivering it reminds us to focus on those goals.

Align the cadence of your eye contact with the rhythm of your thoughts and speech. Put simply, think one person, one thought. We contrast this advice with tips we have heard such as look at each person for three seconds or look at someone until they look away. Remember that the point is to connect.

Virtually, eye contact is tricky, but just as important — and not the impossible barrier it is sometimes labeled. The first thing to remember, of course, is that eye contact virtually is a cheat. You cannot actually look into someone's eyes on the screen and appear to be looking at them, to seem like you are making eye contact. But have no fear. You can still both signal and receive connection.

Locate and love your camera. If you have trouble finding it, move your palm toward your screen until it covers the lens. Once you have found your camera, work to place it at your eye level. Now you have simulated direct eye contact from your end whenever you look into it.

Feel free to look away. When we first started working in virtual space, we felt obligated to look at our camera all the time, and that felt terrible. How could we see people's reactions and actually connect with them rather than just making this false gesture? Then we realized that every time we looked in our camera we were looking at every single person in the room. That meant that if we looked at our camera about 25 percent of the time, we would be simulating eye contact with each "part of the room" about as frequently as we might in an in-person interaction. The rest of the time, we could be free to watch our screens for people's reactions and respond to them. In other words, we learned to make and receive eye contact in two separate stages — giving and receiving independently, but just as effectively.

Use your voice. On the one hand, the hubris of attempting to condense tips about how to use one's voice effectively in a few short paragraphs gives us pause. Our voices are literally instruments that we can spend lifetimes practicing how to use, and many professional singers, actors, and speakers do just that. And those who have specific vocal issues that overtly interfere with their ability to communicate may seek professional, ongoing support to address and remedy those challenges. But that said, for many of us, raising our awareness of some simple aspects of our voice and how to care for it can go a long way in helping us connect with others.

We remember the five aspects of the voice that you can pay attention by using the acronym VTIPS. You can work to build flexibility, range, ease, and health with each one to create a stronger facilitator presence.

Volume

Fundamentally, we want to be able to be heard. That means creating well-supported, energized sound that others do not have to strain to hear. Most of us, most of the time, can be louder than we think when speaking publicly. Let us take a moment to distinguish this from taking up too much space in the room by being bombastic or shouting others down.

We are not talking about being "ugly Americans" or railroading others. We are simply pointing to the ideal level of volume when speaking as a presenter. In many cultures, speaking at a higher volume may be considered rude (especially — let us just name it, for women). But when we want to give the gift of our message, rather than put the onus on the listener to hear what we are saying, sufficient volume is an act of generosity. You are giving your audience the gift of making it easier to pay attention.

In an in-person space, if there is amplification available, use it. People often feel uncomfortable with a microphone; it might seem pretentious or awkward to use one. But please do so. In virtual space, you are usually your own technician. Studies have shown that it is significantly more important for engagement that we can hear than that we can see each other, so do audio checks and invest in decent (it does not have to be wildly expensive) equipment. And check yourself to make sure you aren't too close to the microphone, which causes static and annoys your audience.

Speaking at a slightly higher volume will also often raise your energy level holistically and deepen your breathing, affecting all the other aspects of presence.

Now, having celebrated the value of turning up the volume, we invite you to play with variety here as with all these vocal aspects. As soon as your baseline is set at a comfortable level, turning down the volume for emphasis or to get attention can be very effective.

Tone

Tone in our acronym has come to refer to two separate aspects of our voice. The first is something that most professionals technically call placement. This refers to where the voice resonates. Is it placed in the head, in the mask (we often refer to this as a more nasal sound), in the chest? A well-balanced voice can resonate in an integrated way. If one zone is much more prominent than another, the voice quality will be especially distinctive in a way that might be received as more or less pleasant. Warming up your voice and learning to consciously feel where your voice is placed and resonating can help you create a full and pleasing tone.

The second meaning of tone is the more colloquial meaning related to voice. Does how we say what we are saying match the words we are saying? For example, if I say, "Nice shirt," does my tone convey enthusiasm or sarcasm? Our tone of voice can broadcast warmth or judgment, engagement or boredom. And although a terribly misquoted study by Albert Mehrabian in the popular zeitgeist tends to grossly exaggerate the importance of nonverbal communication, tone does play a critical role in how others evaluate our trustworthiness.[37]

Inflection

Inflection is the movement of pitch or musicality in your voice as you speak. Four standard inflection patterns show up in English.

1. Upward inflection, most commonly found when asking a question. Can you imagine it?

2. Downward inflection, as at the end of a declarative sentence. For example, use this when making a strong, final statement.

3. Sustained inflection, used when, for example, you wanted to set some context, home in on one important detail, and then return to the larger picture. You want to maintain attention without resolving the thought. (Barack Obama is especially good at using this technique.)

---

37 In his 1971 book, *Silent Messages*, Albert Mehrabian shared his research on credibility assessment, which showed that when people perceive misalignment between what is said and non-verbal behavior, they attribute 38% of their assessment of trustworthiness to tone of voice, 55% to body language, and only 7% to the actual content of the words. This research has been wrongly and ubiquitously used to suggest that the content of our communication is only 7% of the value of the message. This is obviously false.

4. Circumflex inflection, when your voice rises and falls, which adds special emphasis or extra emotion to a word.

Facile use of inflection involves appropriate matching of inflection to intention, and as with actual musical compositions, including enough variety to keep things interesting. For example, at an unfortunate moment in the U.S. in 1980s and '90s, we had an epidemic of upspeak in which certain portions of the population began to end every sentence with an upward inflection as if it were a question. This speech pattern violated both the alignment-with-meaning and the switch-it-up recommendations, which resulted in a terribly grating experience. No one, to the best of our knowledge, misses "Valley Speak" or "Valley Girl Speak."

Pitch

Pitch is the notes, whether high or low, of your voice. When thinking about pitch, think both about right fit and range. (Are you noticing a pattern here?) Some of us, because we have gotten explicit feedback or because of cultural norms that have influenced us in one direction or another, have learned to speak habitually in a pitch range that is not quite natural for us. Many men and women have felt that they need to artificially lower their pitch to be perceived as having gravitas. While at first blush, that might seem true, using your voice in a way that is strained or tense can injure it and undermine your presence rather than enhance it. Conversely, many women have also received messages that they must speak in higher-pitched ways to keep from intimidating others.

To find your natural pitch range, take a relaxing breath and they softly say, "mm hmmm" a few times. The pitch range that arises as you vocalize those sounds should put you in the right zone. Try speaking from there and see what emerges.

Speed

Speed is the rate at which you speak. Two tips here: First, most of us can speak more slowly than we would habitually, especially when presenting formally. (This is especially true if you are from the Coastal U.S. or India.) Remember, you know what you are talking about; everyone else is hearing it for the first time. Sometimes, we speak quickly with the intention of taking less time or being efficient. But slowing down can make us easier to understand generally, and can also help us speak more intentionally, and therefore, use fewer words, which in turn may help us with brevity as well. Counterintuitive, right?

Second, variety is your friend. The music analogy is apt here, too. Any speed you choose will devolve into dullness if kept at the same rate for too long. Aim to be Beethoven, not Philip Glass.

In summary, when working with your voice, work to be as easy to listen to as possible: Shoot for clarity and ease, and consider variety your friend.

Pause

(Drumroll, please) A few years ago, Kat came to appreciate the mighty power of the pause when an audience member approached her after a keynote presentation. She had prepared extensively for what had felt like a higher-stakes-than-usual engagement. When the attendee began to praise her for the talk, Kat was eager to hear which points were most effective, but rather than point to any of the content, the participant said, "I was especially impressed by how you answered my question; after I asked it, you took a really long pause and seemed like you were really considering your answer. That meant so much to me. It felt like you were taking me seriously and cared about the issue and my problem."

Pausing can have a powerful on impact your interaction. It can arouse curiosity, deepen a moment of importance, leaving room for laughter or processing, and let you choose words carefully. It can take courage to leave silence, especially in virtual space where we are even less used to it. It takes conscious effort. But when you are able to hold the space without ums and uhs and other filler babble, your presence in the space — and your ability to hold it, therefore, for others as well as yourself — grows exponentially.

That is a lot! Here is a handy reference table to help you remember.

Presenting with Presence

	In Person	Virtual
Body	Get comfortable in the "ready" position: feet under hips, shoulders back, hands at sides, head up, looking forward.	Check in with your breath and body, whether you are sitting or standing. Note the option to hide self-view to manage your focus.
Movement	Support the content and structure by moving only with intention or purpose.	Be aware that all movements are magnified. Adjust your camera, environment, and lighting to highlight your face and minimize distraction.
Hands and Gestures	Gesture with confidence and purpose to illustrate your key points. Bring your hands higher to focus above your shoulders, not below, to frame your face rather than your midsection.	Use slow, deliberate movements. Let people see your hands. Don't hide your face.
Eye Contact	Focus on receiving eye contact, not giving it. Eye contact is about connecting and one of the most powerful status indicators. Don't hold eye contact too long, but don't feel like you have to count an amount of time arbitrarily. A good cadence might be one person, one point.	Look directly into the camera to appear to be making eye contact. Close unnecessary programs and shut off notifications.
Voice	Vary your volume, tone, inflection, pitch, and speed.	Make sure you are easy to hear. Use a high-quality external mic if possible.
Pause	Use pauses to maximize impact and give time for information processing.	Use silence and pauses — they are rare in virtual space, so they can be especially powerful.

Try This: Record Yourself

- In a virtual setting — Get permission from your audience to record a meeting in which you are presenting or facilitating so you can watch the session later to assess how you did.

- In person — Ask a friend to record you on their phone from the back of the room, or simply set your phone at the end of the table as you present. No one needs to even notice.

- It is amazing how much you will be able to see in two to three minutes of video.

  - What do you notice? When were you in command? When did you draw people out effectively? When did you lose people's focus?

  - Which of the skills just presented are you using regularly? Which could you work on?

With today's technology, recording ourselves is easy these days, right? (We will not get into what it was like in the old days — oops, we just did anyway.) What is hard is getting used to watching yourself on video. If you find that uncomfortable at first, you are not alone. Keep at it. It will be the most valuable way of becoming aware of how you use your instrument, and the most efficient way to figure out how to use it more effectively in alignment with your intentions. Why? Because how it feels and how it looks are really different.

Get feedback: Remember that you are only one opinion and not a very objective one at that. Whenever you facilitate, present formally, or even just speak up in a meeting, ask trusted colleagues for feedback. Sound almost as painful as watching a video of yourself? Here are some tips for helping others help you:

Frame your request: Be specific about the kind of feedback you are asking for. For example:

- "I am working on not interrupting others. Could you pay attention today in the meeting and help me notice if and when I do that?"

- "I'm giving a presentation to a big group next week. I know you're going to be there. Would you be willing to give me some feedback on how I was able to fill the space?"

Let them know how you are feeling:

- "Bring it! I want to know everything; I'm dying for feedback!"

- "I'm terrified of doing this. Even getting up there is a win, really. Mostly, I need some moral support."

Equalizing Status

When your goal is to hold focus or establish yourself as a subject-matter expert, these high-status performance tips are the ones to employ. But sometimes we have other goals. Rather than keep the focus on yourself, you may wish to draw others out. In these situations, you might want to deliberately lower your own status. For example, you might want to put those who have less authority or comfort at ease in a brainstorming session, or seek other people's thoughts and feelings when attempting to resolve a conflict.

A good rule of thumb when making status performance choices is that the more you equalize status, the more you create connection and facilitate communication. If you sense that you have higher status compared to others, think about lowering your own and raising theirs. If you think others have higher status, you may need to take on some higher-status behaviors if you want to be respected and establish credibility.

As you practice making conscious status choices, remember that personal presence is just one source of power. Other sources of power, such as formal authority, subject-matter expertise, affiliation, physical characteristics, or socioeconomic position, intersect with status dynamics and will be instrumental in determining the most effective choices in any given moment. The more formal authority you have, for example, the more you may need to engage in low-status behavior to make space for others to feel comfortable speaking up or trusting that you care about their well-being.

An executive coach colleague of ours, Tobey Fitch, tells the story of having dinner with a four-star general, nearly the highest rank in the U.S. Army. Tobey reports that he had never seen anyone listen as attentively or express interest as fully as this officer. As a practitioner in our field, Tobey took the opportunity to ask the general about his status performance: Was it conscious? Absolutely, the general replied. When you carry a formal rank that is so high, and literally wear it on your sleeve, you learn, he said, to compensate with your behavior to equalize the power dynamic and put others at ease. There was never a need for the general to do anything to establish authority — authority entered the room with him by default. On the contrary, he needed to be vigilant about actively putting others at ease if he wished to connect in any way.

Even if we do not officially wear our title on our sleeves, the same dynamics hold true in professional and familial contexts. For one of our clients, we led a series of workshops for midlevel leaders in which each session was kicked off by a different member of the executive leadership team. With each new leader, the impact of their status behaviors and choices became apparent.

When the senior VP of operations, Rashad, kicked off sessions, he took off his suit jacket, rolled up his sleeves, and sat down instead of standing. With a relaxed pose and in a casual tone of voice, he said, "I don't have all the answers. You are on the front lines with our customers and I'm looking for you to bring new ideas."

By lowering his personal status (and raising others; we'll get to that in a bit), Rashad created connection. People were willing to ask questions and interact with him. In fact, one group was so engaged, the session ran over the allotted time. In alignment with his status intelligence performance, rather than simply blaze through the time constraint, Rashad turned to us and asked for permission to continue, saying, "Would it be okay if I took ten more minutes?"

Compare that with the CFO who did not equalize status. He entered the room and immediately sought out the highest-ranking person present. In his kickoff, he would subtly look at his watch while mentioning the board meeting happening in the afternoon. In an attempt to get people talking, he would ask, "Any questions?" and follow up with, "Come on. Don't be shy!" Conversations felt stilted, and he would quickly wrap up by saying, "Well, if there aren't any questions, I'll let you go."

It is astonishing how much influence we can have when we choose these small behaviors deliberately and with awareness of their impact on others, rather than simply, habitually, or with an eye to our own comfort. Here are some tips for how to consciously and effectively raise and lower your own status.

LOW-STATUS BEHAVIORS	HIGH-STATUS BEHAVIORS
Tentative eye contact	Make eye contact
Take up less space (fold arms, hunch shoulders)	Take up space (body and voice)
Touch face or hair	Make statements
Smile continuously	Move with purpose
Seek permission	Listen actively
Respond vs. initiate	Take verbal pauses
Qualify point of view: "I might be wrong, but…"	Offer opinions
	Initiate discussions

Lower your status when you want to…	Raise your status when you want to…
Allow space for others to contribute	Establish credibility
Demonstrate willingness to learn and make mistakes	Convey confidence
Encourage participation	Capture attention
Build trust	Defend others
Show respect and empathy	Settle a debate

Affecting Others

Not only can we shift our own status performances, we can also raise and lower others' status — as Rashad did when he told the group they held the wisdom in the room. When we become attuned to these signals, we key into these small, everyday moves we make. A tiny instruction, compliment, sideways glance, or thumbs-up can have tremendous impact — and why not? In a Darwinian sense, status is the ultimate coin of our realm. It determines who belongs and who doesn't; who eats and who starves; who procreates and whose genes die out. Getting your ideas validated in a meeting may not literally be life and death, but it can sure feel that way. (Or perhaps it is, eh?)

Think back over just the last week of your life. Can you think of any moments when you felt your status drop? Perhaps someone interrupted you during a meeting, or had their head buried in their cellphone as you were attempting to talk to them. Maybe someone you have met multiple times continues to forget your name. Here's a classic: Have you ever offered an idea to receive no response, just to have the same idea celebrated when voiced moments later by someone else? Our guess is, even without an awareness of this language, you felt the impact of these moves.

Virtually everyone we ask says they recognize these behaviors and can identify times when they have felt hurt by them. A more uncomfortable question then arises: Have you ever engaged in any of these behaviors?

Every now and then, when we ask our clients why they perpetrate such behaviors, they confess that they see themselves in cutthroat scenarios vying for power, and that lowering others' status is a deliberate attempt to get ahead. But this is very rare. Usually, people say they commit these transgressions when they are overwhelmed or distracted.

And of course, there is even more complexity to keep track of. Sometimes we may have a habitual or cultural way of interacting that results in lowering others' status — interrupting, for example. In some contexts, where folks identify as "collaborative overlappers," chiming in before someone else finishes feels fine and even supportive — such as New Yorkers over a meal, for example. In others, when "turn-taking" is the conversational norm, as in a presidential debate (Americans may remember Kamala Harris admonishing Mike Pence, "Mr. Vice President, I'm speaking"), it can be terribly insulting.

Here are some tips to keep in mind when making deliberate status relationship choices.

	YOURS	OTHERS
RAISE	• Establish credibility. • Capture attention. • Set limits. • Regain control. • Defend others. • Settle a debate.	• Give credibility. • Model trust-building. • Support their voice. • Offer encouragement/build confidence. • Acknowledge expertise. • Support a culture of mutual respect.
LOWER	• Allow space for others to contribute. • Demonstrate a willingness to learn and make mistakes. • Show respect. • Encourage participation. • Build intimacy. • Support a sense of competence.	• **Use with extreme caution if the choice is to intentionally lower someone else's status.** • Manage a harmful individual. • Regain control in extreme situations.

Try This: Notice Status Lowering

The next time you're in a meeting, having lunch with a friend, or in a conversation with your partner, note the ways we lower and raise others' status.

- Your colleague asks you a question, but then turns to his screen rather than tracking your answer.

- Your partner says, "Are you going to wear that?"

- Your tween child rolls their eyes at the end of every sentence they say to you as if to add "you idiot" at the end.

What do you notice in your environment? How do they make you feel? To receive? To witness? Notice your own status-lowering moves. How do you feel when you are conscious of making those moves? Do you see them land?

Notice status-raising. Small gestures can have an intense positive impact as well, remember. Where can you catch them?

 A heartfelt thank-you

 Deep listening

 A request for advice or help

 A public acknowledgment

How does it feel to receive these? To witness them? When are you habitually excellent at making these choices? Where are there increased opportunities to use the power of conferring status?

Raise someone's status. Now that you possess status consciousness, find an opportunity to use your power for good. Find a chance to raise someone else's status with intention and forethought. What are all the different ways you can come up with to do so? What impact do you notice on not only the other person but yourself? The relationship in an ongoing way? The environment generally? Which new behaviors might you want to try on more often?

The Bottom Line

The truth is no one will never get this right all the time, and although we have been touting the effectiveness we gain when we raise our status awareness and competency, the complexity of all our different sources of power (many of which we can't change), combined with the dozens of things we may have our minds on in any given moment, make it nearly impossible to interact in positive ways every time. But moving our awareness of this core animal power language from unconscious background noise to a conscious focus, and then making thoughtful choices that serve the goal and relationship, can add immensely to our effectiveness.

Chapter Takeaways

- By focusing on the fundamental behaviors of presence (physical and vocal), we significantly enhance our capacity to connect, build trust, and influence others.

- Presence is a reflection of status or power. It's fundamental to how humans evolved as a species. We unconsciously read and respond to status signals. When we're attuned to behavioral signals and the impact it has on others, we can make intentional choices, inspiring trust and connection.

- Equalizing status facilitates communication. If you feel like you have more power than others, consider lowering your status and elevating theirs. Alternatively, if you think others have lower power, adopting some higher-status behaviors can help you gain respect and establish credibility.

- Enhance how people experience you physically and vocally by being mindful of and improving your body language, movements, gestures, eye contact, voice, and pauses

- Practice consciously expanding your behavioral style to better align with your objectives. For example, if you want to encourage others to speak up more in a meeting, practice lowering your status and leaving more space for others to be the focus. If you want to have more influence or focus in a meeting, practice taking up more space physically and vocally.

7 Engage with Story

Enlivens interactions and makes meaning with anecdotes and strong narratives.

I enrich my communication with anecdotes, examples, and personal experiences.

I use narrative structures to aid understanding and recall.

I discern and address "ambient narratives."

I elicit stories from others to enhance insight, connection, and commitment.

Nicola has been sent to Kat's "Storytelling for Influence" course by her manager. She has worked as an engineer at a fast-growing technology company for seven years now and earned the respect of her peers and direct managers, but her career has stalled. Nicola's manager feels it is because somehow Nicola just does not seem to be able to capture the attention of cross-functional partners or get the buy-in of senior leaders in those critical moments when persuasion is most important.

"Everything she says is right," Nicola's manager, Constance, explains. "It's just, well, I don't know … it's just … It feels like it's either too boring and simplistic or too convoluted and hard to follow. She just doesn't know how to tell a good story." Constance is excited for Nicola to work with Kat. These coaching sessions have been offered as a gift to support Nicola's desire for promotion.

When Kat asks Nicola what she hopes to get out of the day, however, she senses that Nicola is less than thrilled to be here.

"Look, I don't mean to be rude," Nicola tells Kat, "but I don't get this whole storytelling business. I don't have time to tell stories, and I don't think most of my colleagues do, either. I just want to give people the most important information as efficiently as possible. Plus, I don't think the best storyteller should have the most influence. I think the best ideas should win out, not the best story."

We have encountered this kind of disconnect before. Storytelling is a hot topic in leadership and communication circles these days, and Constance has almost certainly heard about the value of storytelling as a tool for enlivening presentations, increasing retention, and building credibility. She views it as a holistic tool for building clarity and influence.

Nicola, on the other hand, hears "storytelling" and thinks "fluff." Perhaps she associates the term with the bedtime books she reads to her son. Or, with not much more enthusiasm, the cheesy anecdotes she has heard motivational speakers start with at those all-company offsites she detests.

To put it simply, Constance and Nicola have different stories about storytelling. What is the real deal when it comes to storytelling as a communication tool? Is storytelling just about being entertaining? Can anyone be a good storyteller? Are stories always appropriate or are there specific situations in which stories should or shouldn't be used? What do we even mean by story?

What Is Story?

Let's start by defining our terms. This is not as simple as it sounds: People get PhDs in narratology and argue incessantly about what makes a story a story. (Don't worry, we're not going to do that.) But as you can see from the, ahem, story about Nicola, it is important to clarify what we mean by a story.

On the one hand, our brains are story-making machines, seeking to create meaning from whatever data received. We tend to think of stories as a small subset of our communication — anecdotes, if you will — that people deliberately tell separate from other normal communication. But when we recognize this truth about how our brains work, we can start to see that we are swimming in stories nearly all the time.

We say something in a meeting and the person across the table from us crosses their arms and sighs. We make up a story that they disagreed with what we said or that they thought we were stupid.

We look at a quarterly earnings chart and see a line that goes up and to the right, and we make up a story that our company's recent reorganization has had a positive effect.

We hear a colleague's idea and make up a story about how much positive impact it will have and how much work it will mean for us.

On some level, any time we are receiving data of any kind and connect them into some kind of meaningful whole, we are engaged in a storytelling activity. As Jerome Bruner, the cognitive psychologist, puts it, "Story *is* meaning."[38]

Viewing story as a communication tool at this level allows us to harness its power in much more holistic ways than if we define story as mere anecdotes.

Instead, let us recognize storytelling on three levels.

Level 1: The Anecdote

This, as we have been saying, is what most people commonly think of when they think "story," and it is a rich source of story's powerful reputation. Anecdotes are self-contained narratives often used to explain, engage, or entertain. In much of the storytelling literature, they make up the whole of the storytelling focus.

Level 2: The Key Message

As humans, our natural inclination is to comprehend information through a narrative structure. Consequently, most presentations or conversations inherently possess a narrative thread, comprising a beginning, middle, and end, even if we aren't consciously aware of it.

Sometimes a story will be told about the gathering and information shared; the question is, what will that be? When we consciously recognize and approach your

---

38 Bruner, J. (1990). Acts of Meaning: Four Lectures on Mind and Culture. Harvard University Press.

whole presentation or meeting itself as a story, you can engage listeners more effectively from the beginning by setting the stage, upping the stakes, fleshing out the details, and driving toward our morals.

Level 3: The Ambient Narrative

In addition to any stories we tell, there are countless narratives that already live inside people's heads and in their shared environment. For example, as we started our conversation in this chapter about storytelling, you already had ideas about what a story was and whether it was or was not valuable as a communication tool.

Think about your work contexts: What are the ambient narratives about collaboration? Is it encouraged or is it just for fools who want to be taken advantage of? What about failure? Is it embraced or punished? How do you know? You know because of the ambient narratives, the collection of anecdotes and comments and assumptions that become the cultural norms that become true because they are the stories we tell in our heads, often without even knowing we are telling them. Narratives like these:

 We move fast here. Speed is important.

 Failing fast is all right — rewarded, even, but only certain types of failure.

 We don't have power dynamics here. (At least, that's the ambient narrative in the C-suite).

 Clara is the "smart" one.

Wearing masks is good. (Or wearing masks is silly.)

When we recognize that we are telling our stories — our anecdotes and our key messages — not into blank spaces; not to people with empty, neutral minds; but into ones already teeming with stories and associations that may or may not align with our narratives, then we are more likely to be able to reach our listeners through the noise.

With this view of story, we shift the questions we ask about using story as a communication tool. Instead of these typical questions, we ask these better questions.

Typical Questions	Better Questions
Should I tell stories?	What story should I tell?
Can I tell stories?	How consciously do I craft and deliver the stories I tell?
Will my listeners want to hear a story?	What stories will my listeners arrive with? What story do I want them to leave with?
Is this a good time for a story?	What is the best story for this audience, at this moment, for this goal?

Becoming Better Storytellers

Don't get us wrong. The fact that storytelling is an innate capacity does not mean that we cannot improve our storytelling prowess through strategic practice. When you sat in on eight meetings in one day and heard fifteen different presentations, it's the good stories that usually stick in your mind, right?

Although it may be true that we are all making up stories all the time, what separates effective storytelling communication from pedestrian information transfer is where the burden of the meaning-making is placed.

Great storytellers engage their unconscious narrative processes consciously. They choose their stories deliberately, with more range and flexibility, and guide their listeners so the stories those listeners are likely to make up are aligned with their intentions as speakers. Good storytelling means creating and communicating narratives that feel complete, compelling, memorable, and satisfying.

What Makes a Story Compelling and Memorable?

Nicola has an aversion to storytelling as a communication tool partly because she has been exposed to what we call random anecdote spraying. When people hear that storytelling is a powerful way to engage with others, and they misinterpret storytelling to mean an add-on anecdote, it can be way too easy to fall into the trap of using storytelling only as extraneous, fluffy, or unnecessary nice-to-have extra content.

Just like hearing a bad joke can make people wary of using humor, sharing irrelevant stories or random anecdotes with no relation to the agenda topic or goal has given storytelling a bad name. Too many slides and rambling meetings only make things worse.

Here is what makes stories valuable rather than irrelevant and annoying.

They Make a Point

When using storytelling to influence, educate, or inspire others, be clear about what your message is before you begin. In TED Talk terms: What is *my idea worth sharing?* In storytelling language, what is the moral of my story?

Story	Key Message
The Wizard of Oz	"There's no place like home."
Romeo and Juliet	"Clinging to hate will end in tragedy."
Farmer and Rabbit	"Don't just sit around waiting for a lucky break; do the daily work."
Quarterly sales meeting	"Our strategy is/isn't working." "We need to do _____."
A job interview	"I am the best person for the job."
This chapter	Story *is* meaning: the question is how can you tell your story best, not whether you should tell a story.

As a facilitator or leader preparing to share a story, start by asking yourself, *When I am done speaking, what is the one-sentence insight I want my listener to glean from hearing what I have to say?*

When you have identified the moral of your story, you know what it needs to prove. This immediately reduces the number of things you can appropriately and effectively say from infinite to some manageable, finite number. It becomes a marker on your storytelling map, a North Star, guiding all of your choices.

Story Is Relevant to My Audience

To get your message across to a different audience, tell it through a different story. A new employee needs to hear a different story about the new organizational initiative than the veteran of eighteen years. Your mother needs to hear a different story about how wonderful it will be that you are moving to a new town than your work colleagues do or your spouse who initiated the move.

As we just discussed, your key message provides one point on your map: your desired destination. Now we can place a second point on your map: the spot from which you need to start — where your listeners are. Who will you be trying to communicate with? What do they already know and feel? What assumptions are they entering the room with? Or put another way, what stories are already in their heads?

Nicola needs to hear a different story about the value of storytelling than her boss does. Even though they may both have the same goals for Nicola, have many similar personal characteristics, and work in the same context, Constance has been exposed to knowledge and experiences that Nicola lacks. Their ambient narratives about storytelling are different.

You are never telling stories in a vacuum to blank slates. Know your message, know your audience. Now you are ready to begin making some choices.

Types of Stories

With these two points in mind, we have narrowed our range of appropriate narratives a fair bit to perhaps dozens of potential choices. At this point, depending on your comfort level and experience with consciously telling stories, you may be having one of two thoughts: "Oof, there are still so many stories I could choose to tell. How will I ever decide?" or "Dozens of potential stories? I can't think of even one!" Whichever end of the spectrum you fall on, here are some story qualities we can look for to help us both harvest stories and choose the most effective option.

Yours and Others: Telling your own stories models vulnerability, credibility, and courage. It showcases originality and ownership. Borrowing others' stories offers you a range of options, gives referred credibility, shows humility, and provides the opportunity to give status to the story owner.

Personal and Professional: Sharing a personal story shows vulnerability and relatability and can be humanizing and connecting as it builds on fundamental human experiences. Professional stories (explicitly about experience at work) give credibility and status, are easily applied, and can help motivate or inspire.

Fact or Fiction: True stories based in fact are good for proving a point and transmitting and reinforcing values. For example, at a busy lunch service at Eleven Madison Park in New York City, a Michelin-starred restaurant co-owned by Will Guidara, a group of tourists lamented that they had not had time to try a traditional New York hot dog during their visit. The idea came to Guidara to bring a hot dog, purchased from a nearby cart, into the restaurant and have it served with Michelin-level garnishes to the tourists. The customers were delighted.

The story was passed down to each employee to emphasize the importance and value of hospitality versus just serving a meal.

Fiction stories are good for engaging imagination and making clear points; you can create whatever details best illustrate your key message. Make sure, when using fictional stories, that you are clear that they are made up, so that you do not undermine trust.

Good examples of the use of fictional stories include case studies for practice in training sessions and future forecasting scenarios, or even fables or myths that capture values or philosophies.

High Fidelity or Low Fidelity: High versus low fidelity refers to how close the content of the story is to the real-life experience of the listeners. For example, if you are telling engineering managers the story of an engineering manager who was able to convince new engineers at a tech company to work on his project, even though there were lots of new product projects that sounded more exciting on paper, then your story is a high-fidelity one. The same story shared with sales managers might be useful to discuss influencing skills, but it will be lower fidelity because the specific context is less exact for their needs. If you tell the story to your teenager to encourage them to ask someone out on a date, it will be even lower fidelity.

Higher-fidelity stories offer relatable content to which the listeners can make easy connections. Low-fidelity stories allow listeners to generalize principles and concepts, and not get distracted by the specifics of their content or unique case.

Positionality

There are two more qualities that we can look at: past/future and positive/negative. When we combine them, we create an especially powerful aspect of story-type choice: positionality.

Examples from the past can clarify a concept, illustrate a process, or prove a point. Stories of the future can illuminate a vision or underscore a warning. Together, the combinations look like this.

	Past	Future
Positive	**Model** Proof of the possibility of success Provide lessons and tips for moving forward	**Vision** Inspiration Clarity of goal
Negative	**Cautionary Tale** Avoid known pitfalls, including inertia. People are often more motivated to avoid risk than to seek reward. Inertia is also a powerful force. These stories can make the case for avoiding inaction.	**Warning** As with cautionary tales, showing people what is at stake can be motivating. These stories can paint a picture of what people have to lose.

Once you homed in on your key message, identified your audience, and chosen a specific approach to your story, it is time to look at the structure.

Stories Must Make Sense

Good stories, like well-designed buildings, rest on strong internal frames. To feel like a story, to really move an audience rather than just relay a series of unrelated data points or events, a story must have a cause-and-effect relationship between those events and some kind of change or transformation. In effective communication, those connections have been made explicit for us. In other words, the teller — that's the author, the filmmaker, the presenter, or the person with whom we are having a conversation — does the connecting work for us. Our brains do not have to do as much work to try to make up the connections or fill in gaps. Good stories hang together. They have internal coherence. Aristotle called this Logos or logical flow.

There are scores of books written about storytelling with titles like *The Six Stories You Must Have Ready to Tell* or *The Only 12 Storytelling Structures in the World* or *Every Story Is the Hero's Journey*. In the West, we are drawn to conflict, and some people say you cannot have a story without it. In Eastern cultures, classic story analysis focuses on twists and integration rather than conflict. We think all of that is more complicated than it needs to be.

At the simplest level, the structure of any story can be articulated in this way.

Something is true	➤	Something shifts	➤	Then something new is true.

Really. That is all you need to have a story. Let's try it out.

You can exercise your "thinking in stories" muscles by practicing this structure. Here is an activity we learned from Micaela Blei, PhD. Fill in these blanks:

I used to think _____. Then _____ happened. Now I think_____.

I used to feel _____. Then _____ happened. Now I feel _____.

I used to be _____. Then _____ happened. Now I am _____.

Example: I used to think working virtually was inefficient and couldn't be done, then the pandemic happened, and everyone started to work from home. Now I think it is possible to be even more productive when working virtually versus working in the office.

See, you are a storyteller!

Is that all there is to it? Yes. And, of course, we can flesh out the story a little more. Let's break down the elements and processes of good story creation.

As we work to craft our stories, we are going to distinguish the narrative structure from the final delivery of our story. In the telling, you most often start at the beginning, although not always. When planning stories, start with the end.

Structure Part 1

Working with a moral that you have identified, and this simple structure, test that your story proves the point you wish to make. Whatever is true at the end of the story should align with your moral or key message. Dorothy is home and happy; Romeo and Juliet are dead; the tortoise beats the hare in the race; the team meets their sales goal.

And once you know your ending, you know that the beginning of your story should contrast with it. Our stories start to look like this:

Story	True at the Beginning	True at the End
Romeo and Juliet	Two families feud endlessly, each convinced that they are in the right.	The most beloved children of each of the families are dead and the true price of the never-ending feud is laid bare.
The Farmer and the Rabbit	A farmer diligently tends his fields every day even though the work is hard and dull.	The farmer's fields are fallow and he has nothing because he has neglected them waiting for more rabbits to just come along.
The quarterly sales meeting	Last quarter, we didn't reach our targets, so we discussed implementing this new approach	This quarter, we made our numbers!
The team offsite	Our team culture has felt competitive and exclusionary.	Our vision is everyone feels included and valued.
A job interview	When I was a new manager, eight years ago, I was shy about giving feedback to more senior leaders.	I recognize my external viewpoint is valuable, even to the most experienced practitioner.
This chapter	Storytelling might seem like a specialized form of communication that feels daunting or unimportant to master.	Good storytelling is foundational to good communication, and ubiquitous. It's easy to achieve awareness of just a few tools and concepts.
Your story	???	???

By now, you may have thought, "True, shift, something else true — hmm. That sounds suspiciously like beginning-middle-end." And you wouldn't be wrong. But the magic of this little formula lies in the shift.

When we can identify and highlight a *clear moment* of change in our stories, our messages become stronger and more affecting, and our audiences are more engaged and convinced. The middle isn't just stuff happening. It is stuff happening that causes the end to be different from the beginning.

These shifts sometimes build to a very clear moment of realization or transformation.

 Beginning state: Kirsten used to be afraid she was too selfish to be a mother.

 Shift: Then she saw her daughter's face for the first time.

 End state: Now she knows she would give up anything, including her own life, for her child.

Sometimes shifts are more of a process.

 Beginning state: Our team was competitive and exclusionary.

 Shift: By examining our unconscious biases and building psychological safety, we changed our practices and norms.

 End state: Now we are inclusive, and everyone feels valued.

Regardless, you can identify the shift by asking the question, what ultimately caused the change from the beginning state to the end state? And when you have all three elements, you have a stable foundation for a story.

Story	True at the Beginning	Shift	True at the End
Romeo and Juliet	Two families feud endlessly, each convinced that they are in the right.	The son and daughter of the two respective families fall in love.	The most beloved children of each of the families are dead and the true price of the never-ending feud is laid bare.
The Farmer and the Rabbit	A farmer diligently tends his fields every day even though the work is hard and dull, until one day he sees a rabbit crash into a tree and die right in front of him, which affords him meat for a delicious meal.	Because he is so delighted by the good fortune of finding the rabbit, he spends all his time waiting for rabbits to slam into trees, rather than continuing to tend his fields.	The farmer's fields are fallow, and he has nothing because he has neglected them waiting for more rabbits to just come along.
The quarterly sales meeting	Last quarter, we didn't reach our targets, so we discussed implementing this new approach.	We implemented the new approach.	This quarter, we made our numbers!
A job interview	When I was a new manager, eight years ago, I was shy about giving feedback to more senior folks.	A very senior employee told me how some feedback he had asked me for had helped him be more successful.	Since then, I have believed that I have value to offer even more experienced people on my team.
This chapter	When some people are introduced to the topic of storytelling, they may have stories in their heads that conjure resistance to the idea of telling more stories.	After exploring some concepts and tools, they realize there is already a fantastic inner storyteller just waiting to be unleashed.	From then on, they tell stories in conscious and deliberate ways to enhance their influence and build connection and trust.
Your story	???	???	???

Structure Part 2

Taking our understanding of story structure just one step further, with just one more layer of complexity, will help us create robust, complete, and satisfying narratives every time. Your most popular and effective story-crafting tool is the Story Spine.

The Story Spine was first devised by Kenn Adams to help improvisers collaboratively — and spontaneously — create well-made plays. Since then, largely through the work of Kat and her colleagues, it has been adopted by Pixar animators, as well as storytellers, speakers, and leaders across the globe. In short, the Story Spine offers a series of simple prompts that together provide a scaffolding for all the stages of a well-told story

When a story contains all the sections in the Spine, it feels complete to us. This is not to say that when we actually tell our stories, we will literally use the words of the Spine to start our sentences. Nor does it even mean we will always present our stories in Spine order. But as we start to construct the logical narrative structure of our story, the Spine acts as excellent scaffolding to help us discover the necessary and sufficient elements.

Let's apply it to a familiar story and unpack those jobs.

Once upon a time ... Every day ...	**Platform** This is the introduction to the setting and characters in the story. The exposition. It gives listeners the context and sets the stage.	Once upon a time ... there was a farmer who had to work very hard to make a living from his fields. Every day ... he tended his crops, planting, watering, sowing, and reaping, even though the work was hard and dull.
But one day ...	**Catalyst** This is the instigating event, the reason that the story is being told, the "why today is different" moment.	But one day ... a rabbit, frightened by a bird of prey overhead, dashed out of the underbrush, slammed into a tree, and died right in front of the farmer.
Because of that ... Because of that ... Because of that ...	**Consequences** This is the main body of the story; what ensues from the catalytic event. Each event leads to another event, building suspense and tension.	Because of that ... the farmer had a delicious stew for dinner that night and a rabbit skin to sell at the market that week without having to do very much work at all. Because of that ... he thought, "This rabbit thing is great!" and waited by the tree for more rabbits rather than tending his fields. Because of that ... his crops died.
Until finally ...	**Climax** The clincher. The moment for which we all wait!	Until finally ... the farmer had nothing to eat and nothing to sell.
Ever since then ... The moral of the story is ...	**Resolution** The conclusion. *Not always explicitly included, should be clear when seeking to influence*	And ever since then ... he has realized the foolishness of waiting around for rabbits rather than tending to his fields. And the moral of the story is ... put in the work; don't sit around waiting for lucky breaks.

That's all there is to it. You can sense how organic the Spine feels, right?

Try This: Story Spine

Take your favorite movie or classic fairy tale and see if you can map it to the Spine. It is a great way to start to get foundational narrative story structure into your bones.

Now let's use the Spine to build a story that we might use in a professional context. Imagine I am a senior partner with a global consulting firm. I am meeting with a client who is attached to continuing to run his business the way he always has, even though the external landscape has changed significantly. I believe he may open up to my ideas if I share the story of a CEO I worked with a few years ago who was in a similar situation. (This will be a true/professional/high-fidelity/model story I will be attempting to craft.)

Once upon a time ... Every day ...	**Platform** This is the introduction to the setting and characters in the story. The exposition. It gives listeners the context and sets the stage.	**Once upon a time** ... there was a very successful CEO who had been at the helm of the organization he founded for over a decade. **Every day** ... he committed to its success with every ounce of his energy, getting involved with every decision, overseeing every product launch personally, and making sure that the work culture was designed exactly in alignment with his values and preferences.
But one day ...	**Catalyst** This is the instigating event, the reason that the story is being told, the "why today is different" moment.	**But one day** ... there was a global pandemic and everyone was forced to work remotely.

	Consequences This is the main body of the story; what ensues from the catalytic event. Each event leads to another event, building suspense and tension.	Because of that ...the employees demonstrated that they were capable of staying connected, motivated, and doing great work from home. **Because of that** ... the CEO was forced to re-examine his long-held belief that allowing people to work remotely would ruin the organization's culture and productivity. **Because of that** ... he struggled, because he realized that his desire to have people back in the office was more of a personal preference than a business necessity.
Because of that ... Because of that ... Because of that ...		
Until finally...	**Climax** **The clincher. The moment for which we all wait!**	**Until finally** ... he was able to see himself as separate from the business in a way he hadn't before.
Ever since then ... The moral of the story is ...	**Resolution** The conclusion. *Not always explicitly included, should be clear when seeking to influence*	**And ever since then** ... he has been asking, "Where else do I need to detach and step away to let the business mature?" **And the moral of the story is** ... sometimes we can have a clearer view from a distance.

As you can see, the Spine may seem simple — even restrictive — but just like spines in human bodies, it can support nearly infinite variety. Note that the Spine is descriptive rather than prescriptive, aiming to capture the core structure of what our brains recognize as complete, coherent narrative. It acts, therefore, as a cognitive tool for constructing and evaluating the logical stability and completeness of your message.

Try This: Craft a Story

Using our Craft a Story template at the end of this chapter, build a story for a real-life situation in which you would like to have more influence.

Stories Engage Our Emotions and Imaginations

By now, you have a strong, clear, scalable message. And in some situations, the version you have created might be perfect just as it is (minus a "once upon a time" or two). But there are a few more ways we might want to play with our stories to make them even more appropriate for their contexts, memorable, and compelling.

We already mentioned Aristotle's first element of effective argument — Logos, or Logic — when we discussed the Spine. His other two famous elements are, of course, Pathos and Ethos — emotion and character. Pathos requires little clarification. When we feel emotionally engaged in a narrative, we remember the information conveyed longer and are more motivated to act on its key message. Ethos, in Aristotelian terminology, literally meant the character of the individual speaking, and more broadly, the credibility or values inherent in the message.

If structure is the first *S* of storytelling, here are four more *S*'s to make a full list of five.

Specifics

Genius is in the details, it is said, and this is certainly true of great stories. Once the structure of your story is set, it is time to decide where to add detail, description, and explanation to make your story the most understandable, memorable, and convincing. The Spine can be thought of as the action of your story or the essential narrative thread. Once that is in place, color can be added.

What Can Be Described	How Elements Can Be Described
• People	• Images/imagery
• Environments	• Metaphors
• Emotions	• Charts/Graphs
• Thoughts/Memories	• Dialogue
• Data	• Acting it out

Where, when, and how much description is appropriate depends on:

 How much time you have

The medium you tell your story through (conversation, formal presentation, print, audio, video, for example)

There is no general rule about how much description to add or where to add it. The art of storytelling is to select the appropriate type and quantity of description tailored to both the specific situation and audience. To improve your coloring muscles, do this:

 Get to know when you are coloring and when you are advancing in your narrative. Hint: If your Spine stays coherent and complete without a specific detail included, that detail probably acts as color. If you can ask, "What happened next?" before a sentence, it is probably an advancing statement.

Know yourself. Do you have a preference? Some of us love to color. If we pay attention, our listeners will send us signals that we should be advancing, like nodding vigorously or saying Yes, yes, okay. (If you are Kat's and Therese's spouses, they literally say, "Advance.") Others of us advance efficiently but could stand to color more. You will know your listeners are seeking more color if they are asking questions, looking confused, or leaning forward with rapt attention.

 Exercise each skill independently. Set a timer or work with a partner to arbitrarily move back and forth from description to action. Strengthen your comfort with each without worrying about choosing the appropriate move at any given time.

 Scale your story appropriately. Once you are capable of adding color where and whenever it is called for, you can make the choice to color or advance, not just in the preparation phase, but at the moment, responsively. Think of the Spine as the most essential information and then layers of color as useful and nice-to-know elements that you can add, depending on how much time you have and who you are speaking with.

How Much to Say

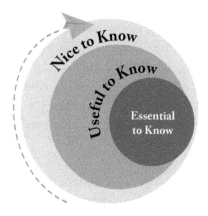

Show, Don't Tell

Rather than simply telling us that someone in your story is strong or courageous or rude or foolish, share the observable behaviors that prove that description. The more you can use your description to let your listeners experience the sensory and emotional aspects of your story, the more you will create a vivid impact.

Stay in the moment of the action you are recounting, especially when you are telling personal stories. If you let us know what the people in the story are thinking and feeling as the events unfold, then we, the listeners, can experience those events along with the characters. The moments that surprised you will surprise us!

Surprise

Speaking of surprise, don't be fooled into thinking that because you have a strong logical structure for your story, your story must be predictable or boring. Just the opposite. Once you are clear about all the elements of your story and how they fit together, you can make conscious choices about what to reveal and what to hold back, how to build suspense and create a satisfying climax that supports a convincing and memorable moral.

Here are some ways to include surprise in your stories:

 Play with time. You don't always have to start your story at the beginning. "Our hero is hanging from a branch over a pit of hungry alligators. How did he get here?" Or "We think we have a way we can save you $100 million annually. Shall we explain what you would have to do?"

 Ask yourself:

- Where is the hook or most compelling moment to start?
- What will raise a question and pique my listeners' interest?
- Start there and fill in the gaps before and after.

 Resist foreshadowing: Alternatively, sometimes you want to avoid getting ahead of yourself. When describing a problem, for example, take time to really let your listeners feel and understand the depth of it before presenting your solution. This is not always the best choice, but when going for surprise, it can't be beaten. Sometimes, you might even want to misdirect. Did things turn out fine? How might you want to highlight how they might have gone terribly wrong?

Share Yourself

When telling a story, whether it's your own or someone else's, help people understand why it matters to you. You're the credibility factor, the ethos, in your story. Your emotional investment is what creates a connection and makes your audience feel, adding that emotional appeal, or pathos. Both of these qualities come most from how you tell your story once you have set the foundational structure. Let us see what matters to you, where you are vulnerable, where fierce. Why are you the best person to share this story? How will this story help us understand not just information, but you?

Example

My audience:	New people leaders
What stories could I tell to support my main point?	*Don't avoid a tough feedback conversation.*
What's the main point I want my audience to take away?	• *A situation where a manager was inconsistent in giving feedback* • *A successful leader who gave feedback* • *What it's like for direct reports when they don't get enough feedback*

	Platform The starting condition (status quo; the routine)	*Tom was a well-liked leader of the software development group. He was known for creating a positive and encouraging team environment. He didn't like conflict and avoided confrontation.*
	Catalyst The break in the routine	*The team was high performing except for a couple of team members who weren't pulling their weight. He couldn't afford a lack of productivity given the tight timelines for the new product releases and he didn't want to make the situation any worse than it was.*
	Consequences Because of that... Because of that... Because of that...	*Tom tried to fix the problem by reassigning some of the tasks to play to everyone's strengths instead of addressing the problem directly. The poor performers didn't get the direct feedback, and because of that, the high performers had to pick up the slack and became resentful.*
	Climax The lasting change or pivot	*Eventually, a trusted colleague told Tom that by not giving direct feedback to the poorer performers, the rest of his team was losing confidence and respect in him and put overall team performance at risk. Tom thought he was fixing the problem but was actually compounding it.*
	Resolution The lesson or key take-away	*It was a light bulb moment for Tom. Avoiding tough conversations was eroding team trust in him as the leader. It gave him the confidence to have a direct feedback conversation and hold people accountable.*

My audience:		
What stories could I tell to support my main point?		
What's the main point I want my audience to take away?		
	Platform The starting condition (status quo; the routine)	
	Catalyst The break in the routine	
	Consequences Because of that... Because of that... Because of that...	
	Climax The lasting change or pivot	
	Resolution The lesson or key take-away	

As we exercise and integrate these techniques, we have only begun to scratch the surface of the power of story. Beyond storytelling, skilled facilitators listen for and draw stories out from others. We design and run formal and informal story-sharing activities. We use narrative structures as visioning and problem-solving structures, icebreakers, learning aids, and diagnostic tools. But even by simply beginning to *think* in story, you will have unlocked a profound capacity to increase your value in any interaction. You will have become a meaning maker, and by so doing, you will be able to make everything clearer, more memorable, and more compelling for everyone in the room.

Chapter Takeaways

- Our brains are inherently storytelling machines. Meaning is co-created by the speaker and the listener.

- Good storytelling is about creating and communicating narratives that feel complete, compelling, memorable, and satisfying.

- Stories do not exist in a vacuum communicated to blank slates. People already have their own stories and ideas (their ambient narratives) that should be identified and considered when planning your communication.

- Start by identifying the moral of the story. It becomes the guiding marker, influencing all your storytelling decisions.

- A well-structured story starts with something is true, then something shifts and something new is true.

- The Story Spine, through a series of simple prompts, acts as a scaffolding for all the stages of a well-told story.

- Add description and detail to your story to emotionally engage your listener and increase retention and impact.

8 Listen

Seeks to connect deeply with others, hearing both the spoken and unspoken, and supporting them where they are.

I demonstrate active listening by paying attention not just to words, but also to intentions, values, and emotions.

I proactively seek out and acknowledge all points of view, even when they differ from my own.

I actively summarize and integrate the reactions and insights of others.

I spark meaningful interactions by asking thought-provoking questions that encourage genuine participation and foster deeper engagement.

Kari didn't expect to be the hero of the meeting. With a room full of technical experts, the pressure was on to find a fix to get the production line back on track. Every creative idea was shot down quickly as unrealistic or not feasible. Thirty minutes in and no closer to a solution, Kari called a time-out and said, "What if everyone could withhold their assumptions, reserve judgment for a moment, and listen a little deeper to the ideas first?"

The call to listen triggered the group to hear out ideas more fully before critiquing them. Before long, a viable solution was found. After the meeting, Jeff came up to

Kari to thank her for the reset and she replied, "I knew if we did more listening, we'd find a way."

Of all the contributions, it's the skill of listening that exceptional facilitators rely on most. And it's really hard. When our primary role is to serve others (clients, our boss, direct reports, peers, a friend), listening well means putting them first. It means receiving information before giving it and allowing that information to inform how to respond. It requires us to shelve our own agendas and opinions (temporarily) and stay open before judging or reacting. It requires us to consider the context and situation and listen below the surface, beyond just the facts to emotions, intentions, and values. Interactions where everyone feels heard, respected, and understood do not happen by accident.

We are not wired to be great listeners:

 We lose focus. We hear "faster" than the typical rate of speech so our mind wanders.[39]

 We spend about 47 percent of our time thinking about something other than what we are doing.[40]

 We make assumptions and have filters (bias), so we often misunderstand what is being said.[41]

 Sometimes we do not *want* to listen, especially when we don't like what we are hearing.

39 Hargie, O. (2022). *Skilled Interpersonal Communication: Research, Theory and Practice*. Routledge.
40 Killingsworth, MA, and Gilbert, DT. A wandering mind is an unhappy mind. Science. 2010 Nov 12;330(6006):932. doi: 10.1126/science.1192439. PMID: 21071660.
41 Tsai, W. (2020). Reality is Constructed by your Brain. Neuroscience Institute, Stanford University.

We think we have heard it all before, so we jump to conclusions.

Think about it. Most of us have never been formally taught how to listen well. It's not usually taught at home. In school, listening often means hearing and comprehending content (while tuning out your annoying classmate). If you were lucky, good listening was modeled by a family member, friend, or mentor, and you felt the benefit of being acknowledged, understood, and validated. Sadly, most of us operate in a world where there is a listening deficit — people talking over one another or half-listening while attempting to multitask. By the time we get into our first jobs, we mistake hearing for good listening.

Most of us overestimate our ability to truly listen effectively. There's a price to pay to be an above-average listener. It requires attention, concentration, and a willingness to give up control by temporarily putting our thinking on hold. It's worth the "price" when the goal is to build rapport, influence, show respect, or problem-solve. When people feel genuinely heard and understood, they say more, which leads to more informed decision-making and better outcomes.

We bet you are a pretty good natural listener when you are genuinely curious and interested. If you were in the middle of a project and your boss interrupted and said, "Hey, I have some news about how the bonus calculation is changing," you might stop in your tracks and be all ears.

I'm Listening When I Am ...	I'm Not Listening When I Am ...
Seeking answers	Busy/Rushed
Interested or motivated	Uninterested
Looking for support	Distracted
Curious and open-minded	In a disagreement or not seeing the value of the speaker's point

On the flip side, when in a hurry, uncomfortable, preoccupied, or not invested in the topic, we tune out. And let's be honest, aren't we all more rushed, distracted, and stressed these days? There's a cost for not listening. Think of all the times you experienced a misunderstanding or miscommunication because people — including yourself — barely listened or assumed understanding. Now, imagine how much time and energy could be saved by better listening.

If you want to advance your listening skills, consider three questions. We'll introduce them and then take a deeper dive.

Who am I listening to? There is always something competing for your attention. At any given moment, your focus might be on the speaker, the chatter in your head, other people, or the environment. What tends to grab more of your attention and what effect is it having on people?

What am I listening for? Words don't always carry the full weight of their meaning. If we take words at face value, we may miss the nuances of what's really being said and never get to the deeper meaning.

How am I listening? You can listen as a friend or listen as a foe. Being open, curious, and interested are the hallmarks of those who listen as a friend and gets rewarded with better problem-solving and greater rapport. Listening as a foe means filtering for errors, faults, and disagreements, and gets "rewarded" with festering problems because people will hesitate to tell you more. Deciding how to listen shapes the outcome.

Who Am I Listening to?

With his eyes affixed to the screen, Theo took in the board's question about the budget for the annual fundraiser. He nodded, maintained eye contact, and gave the appearance of listening. At one point, their voices transformed into the sounds of the adult characters from the Peanuts cartoon in an indecipherable cacophony of sound.[42]

If we could peer inside Theo's head, we would notice all his attention turned inward. Like a voice-over track in a movie, he was saying to himself, *I better get this right* and *I'd love to see them try to pull off a gala on a shoestring budget*! His inner voice acted as a saboteur, distracting him from the people on the call and redirecting his focus to himself. He was only jolted back into the conversation when someone casually referred to him by name.

Just as our inner dialogue can draw us away from listening, it can also enable us to be more present and actively engaged. For instance, self-talk like, *Keep listening, Stay curious,* or *It's not about me right now* would turn attention back to the speaker.

---

42 Fun fact: Fans of Peanuts will be bemused to know it's a trombone with the rubber end of a toilet plunger over the instrument's bell!

A Non-Listener's Mindset	A Listener's Mindset
"I already know what they are going to say." "I don't have time for this." "What am I supposed to say next?" "They are wrong." "If they would just stop talking ..."	"I want them to feel heard and understood." "They are more likely to hear my point of view if I listen to them first." "Listen beyond the facts. What do they value or care about?" "I wonder where I have gaps in my understanding or knowledge?"

The good news is you get to choose where your attention goes. In the "Manage Yourself" chapter, we explore this silent, internal soundtrack and how to manage it so it serves you and the situation effectively.

Try This: Build a Listener's Mindset

Think about an upcoming conversation where it is important for you to be an active listener.

Write down self-talk that will support you in being fully present.

Repeat that self-talk during the meeting. Think about what will help you recall it when you need it.

Beyond our thoughts, there is a symphony of other sounds and stimuli we could be listening to that together complete the soundscape of our current situation.

Our bodies: The rumbling of an empty stomach, distraction of a sore back from an uncomfortable chair, desperate need for a bathroom break

Our environment: The room temperature, a cramped conference room next to the elevator, a home office with our dog barking in the background, a retreat center with a view of the mountains

Other people: The distraction of two people whispering to each other, someone rolling their eyes, people not turning on their cameras during a video call.

What should you listen to when bombarded by attention-grabbing options? Consider what will enable you and the group to stay present and fully engaged. For instance, if people's eyes are nodding shut, call a break. If you see people shivering in a cold room, address the temperature needs. If you notice body language that reflects disagreement, call it out. What *doesn't* work is ignoring the signals and powering through a meeting without addressing them.

You might be thinking, *Okay, this is all great, but what happens when my mind wanders?* It's normal for attention to drift. As we said earlier, 47 percent of the time, we're not paying attention to what's happening in front of us.[43] It happens to all of us. Therese was facilitating a virtual team meeting when, out of the corner of her eye, she noticed an incoming email she was anxiously awaiting all day. You can guess where her attention went!

Add the reality that only 2.5 percent of us are effective at multitasking.[44] When our brains are constantly jumping between tasks, especially when attention is required, we're less efficient and more prone to mistakes.

---

43 Killingsworth, M.A., and Gilbert, D.T. A wandering mind is an unhappy mind. *Science*. 2010 Nov 12;330 (6006):932. doi: 10.1126/science.1192439. PMID: 21071660.
44 Leland, A., Tavakol, K., Scholten, J., Mathis, D., Maron, D., and Bakhshi, S. The Role of Dual Tasking in the Assessment of Gait, Cognition and Community Reintegration of Veterans with Mild Traumatic Brain Injury. *Mater Sociomed*. 2017.

What can we do about it? Start by noticing when you zone out and what contributes to it. At the moment your mind begins to ruminate over the to-do list and not what's happening in front of you, gently redirect your thoughts to the speaker. Supportive self-talk might sound like this: *The to-do list has to wait. If I give 100 percent of my attention to this conversation, I won't need to ask for clarification later.*

More proactively, identify the things that distract you or cause your mind to wander, and look for ways to minimize them. For instance, silence your devices or move away from the distractions. If you need a bathroom break, ask for it. Chances are others do, too. If you need a minute to quiet the barking dog or greet the kids coming home from school, request a temporary pause, if possible. If the nonverbal signals people are giving in the meeting tell you no one has bought into the idea, recognize it and call it out. If back-to-back meetings are causing information overload, try creating a small buffer between meetings to recharge and recenter yourself.

Many mindfulness apps and online courses can help you learn to stay present and centered. Here's one activity to get you started.

Try This: Mindful Listening Exercise

Invite a friend to speak about a topic for three to four minutes. The listener's role is to be mindful. Do not interrupt the speaker. As the listener, take notice of your tendencies:

- How strong is your urge to problem-solve, offer advice, or share your own story?
- What are you silently saying to yourself?
- What assumptions might you be making?
- What are some of the unspoken qualities of the interaction?

With new awareness of the ways to support yourself to be a ready listener, you are ready to explore the next question: What am I listening for?

What Am I Listening for?

In a famous Harvard University experiment,[45] participants were asked to watch a video of a group tossing a ball and count how many times they passed it to each other. At one point in the video, a person in a gorilla suit strolls by in the background. Afterward, when asked if they spotted the gorilla, around half of the participants said they had missed it all together. We miss a lot of details in our environment, and we have no idea that we are missing so much.

Listening well is the key that unlocks the unspoken dynamics of a situation. It goes beyond relying solely on words and delves into the subtleties of body language, the symphony of sighs and silences, and the hidden currents of emotions that ripple beneath the surface. It explores the depths of what remains unsaid — the unarticulated

45 Simons, D. J., and Chabris, C. F. (1999). Gorillas in Our Midst: Sustained Inattentional Blindness for Dynamic Events. *Perception* 28(9), 1059–1074. https://doi.org/10.1068/p281059.

needs, the untold ambient stories, and the concerns of the group that shape the fabric of our interactions.

Here's the good news: listening well is a learned skill. Like a highly trained doctor who detects the faintest symptom before a heart attack, a skilled food critic identifying every ingredient in a dish by taste alone, or a seasoned firefighter who pulls her team out of a burning building moments before it collapses, you, too, can learn to listen so well that you support your colleagues by understanding their needs before they're even aware of them.

When Our Perception May Not Match Reality

 Assuming your nerves are apparent to everyone in the meeting

 Overestimating (or underestimating) people's knowledge or experience

 Interpreting silence to mean everyone agrees

 Believing that participants share the same beliefs and values

Our capacity to observe and listen tends to diminish when we're in nerve-racking situations, facing objections, or being caught off guard. In those moments, our attention often turns inward, fixating on our own needs and emotions, which hijacks our ability to perceive and accurately interpret what's happening around us. It's known as egocentric bias.[46] Our brain often behaves like

46 Samuel, S., Frohnwieser, A., Lurz, R., and Clayton, N. S. (2020). Reduced egocentric bias when perspective-taking compared with working from rules. *Quarterly Journal of Experimental Psychology* 73-9, pp. 1368–1381.

a master storyteller, filling in gaps in our perception to create a cohesive narrative. When we are absorbed in our own needs and emotions, we can misunderstand or misinterpret the intentions and behaviors of those around us.

When it comes to the spoken word, there are often multiple layers to what people tell us. When we listen more deeply, we get a more complete understanding that enables us to consider how to proceed in any conversation. We call it deep D.I.V.E. listening (Data/Facts, Intentions, Values, Emotions).

A popular improvisational theater game highlights the kinds of offers we can listen for. (In improv parlance, an offer is anything my partner says or does.) In the game of Telephone, we ask one person to share a meaningful experience in a minute or two. They tell their story to another person while two other people wait outside so they won't hear. Then, one by one, the listeners become the storytellers, with instructions to tell the story to the next person as exactly as possible, as if they were a video recording. Just as in the children's game, key elements of the story are lost, and people realize how important and difficult it is to listen not just for information but all elements.

Leon arrived five minutes late to the contract meeting. He said in a weary tone, "I'm really sorry, but the director of procurement kept me late." As he flipped through his notebook, he sighed and said in a soft tone, "I just wish I could get a handle on all these contracts. I am always playing catch-up."

Let's unpack that moment and listen on multiple levels. For now, these are assumptions until confirmed by Leon.

Data/Facts: Leon is running behind. He would prefer to be more up to speed on the contract.

Intentions: Leon wants to be ahead of the game instead of late to the party.

Values: He cares about time, inclusion, accuracy, and efficiency.

Emotions: He is weary, frustrated, and feeling behind.

If the situation is a straightforward, stand-alone transaction, acknowledging the facts and moving on might suffice. But more often, when there is emotion in the message, or the relationship is important, deeper-level listening builds rapport and helps problem-solve. For instance, if Leon is continually excluded from the early stages of contract negotiations, problems will fester unless the issue is first understood and then acted upon.

Deep D.I.V.E. listening requires us to be astute observers and pick up on what's being said — and what's *not* being said — so we can uncover true motivations, moods, interests, or concerns. Nonverbal communication tends to convey more emotions than what we verbalize.[47]

---

47 Communication in the Real World: n Introduction to Communication Studies. Provided by University of Minnesota Libraries Publishing through the eLearning Support Initiative. License: CC BY-NC-SA: Attribution-NonCommercial-ShareAlike.

DEEP D.I.V.E. LISTENING

• Data/facts (budget, timeframe, measurable actions taken)
• Intentions (the primary driver for the action)
• Values (personal, business)
• Emotions (anger, anxiety, excitement)

Let's consider another story.

Jayla was presenting the new sales targets when she noticed Sam and Vanessa sitting silently with their arms folded and blank stares on their faces. Occasionally, she caught them glancing at each other knowingly. She knew the new targets were aggressive, but she felt they were achievable. Moreover, the new targets introduced the potential for higher bonuses, which would be good news for everyone. She asked if there were any questions about the new targets, but there were none. She called on Sam and Vanessa, but they gave clipped responses: "No, we got it." "It's fine."

With no questions, she ended the meeting, thinking, "Well, that went better than expected!" Later, she replayed the meeting in her head and wondered if it really went well or if she missed something. She was only listening on the surface.

When nonverbal behaviors are incongruent with a person's words, ignoring them or putting the onus on the person to "just tell me what you really think" does not work, especially when you hold more power.

If we could coach Jayla in the moment, we would encourage her to listen to the silence more deeply. We would suggest she share her observation on nonverbals to surface values and emotions. For instance, she could say, "I am noticing the blank expressions and silence. I'm wondering what you're thinking. What is happening for you right now?"

If the team has a good relationship with Jayla and feels safe, they might divulge a number of things, such as issues with how realistic the target is (intentions), a worry about fairness and equity of the plan (values), feeling disappointment that she did not negotiate a lower target for the team or even excitement for the potential of a bigger bonus (emotions), and the list goes on. None of that is disclosed to her if she listens on a surface level. Even if she can't change the target, the team might feel more respected and heard if she would just listen more deeply.

Their Body Language	Their Words	Deep D.I.V.E. Listening
Looks down, voice quivers, tearing up	"It's fine."	"It doesn't seem fine. Help me understand what you're thinking."
Silent, rolls eyes, arms crossed	"Whatever."	"I am getting the sense that you're resigned to the idea. Is that accurate? How come?"
Blank stare, look away, sighing	Silence (no words)	"I'm not sure how to read your silence. What's behind it?"

The bottom line is that listening well requires a look beyond words to intentions, values, feelings, and emotions.

Try This: Deep D.I.V.E. Listening

Ask a friend to talk with you about a subject that is meaningful and important to them. After ten minutes, stop the conversation and silently jot down what you captured. Then share it with your friend to see how accurate you were in capturing data/facts, intentions, values, and emotions. If you weren't hitting the mark, try it again or switch roles.

- What data/facts did I hear?

- What am I interpreting as their intention? What do they want?

- What do I perceive as their beliefs that guide their thinking or actions?

- What feelings are they expressing?

Verbalize Your Understanding — Restate

One of the most effective skills for ensuring you get to deeper layers is restating. It's a way to bring the picture into focus by expressing your understanding of the other person's perspective. The way you acknowledge what a person shares — especially when the topic is sensitive — tells them and the group a lot about you. Is it safe to go deeper, and be open and honest? Are you really interested? Will you hear my side of the story?

Restating is a simple and effective way to make sure you and the other person share the same understanding. Effectively catching what people say quickly builds credibility and trust. It is stating, in your own words, the essence of what the speaker is saying or feeling.

It's simple but not easy. It's an advanced listening skill because it's not often our first choice. We lean on other behaviors instead, like agreeing or disagreeing, stating an opinion or counterpoint. Yet, restating is a fast and effective way to build credibility with a person. When they believe you understand them, they are more willing to tell you more.

Imagine a conversation between Flora and her boss, Tomas. Flora, who is new to the company, wants to talk with him about the challenges she's facing.

Flora: "I'm really impressed with the talent on the team. Everyone is obviously very smart."

Tomas: "Great. I'm happy to have you on the team."

Flora (in a hesitant tone): "Well, I am finding it pretty hard to get a fair hearing as a new person. There's a lot of 'We tried that before' or 'That may have worked in Latin America, but it won't work in this market.'"

Tomas: "Some people can be a little too blunt and rough around the edges. Everyone means well. There's a lot of experience on this team, and no one wants to repeat the mistakes from the past. Just give it some time."

Flora: "Okay."

What if the conversation ends there? Tomas may think he was helpful in explaining or justifying Flora's experience. He was listening to the facts only. If Tomas was a more advanced listener, tuning into emotions, intentions, values, and power dynamics, he would restate. Let's imagine what would happen if he listened more deeply.

Tomas (restatement): "So, Flora, you're not finding the team to be open to your ideas."

Flora: "No, and people seem more resistant to change than I expected. You brought me here to bring new ideas, but I find myself not even speaking up in team meetings anymore."

Tomas (restatement): "Wow. You're feeling like the group has stifled you."

Flora: "Yes. I'm not sure what's the best approach in this environment. I don't want you to fight my battles for me because I'm afraid it will make it worse. Do you think Adam and Brian will be open to feedback? I'm willing to raise the issue, but I'm worried that I'll come across the wrong way. I don't want to inflame the situation."

As the conversation continues, Tomas has a better understanding of Flora's intentions, values, and emotions. And he recognizes that Flora needs a sounding board and some guidance, not for him to "fix" the problem for her.

When you restate, you validate the speaker, ensuring that you and others have heard them correctly and, in turn, create more safety for others to share.

You might know of someone who went to some old-school listening training and came back sounding like a technique. Every reply starts with a phrase like, "So what I hear you saying is — " Cringe! At best, it sounds inauthentic; at its worst, it can feel condescending. Here's a better, more genuine way of restating.

Make it short: If a person offers a paragraph worth of words, aim for a restatement that is a sentence, keeping the focus on them and not you. For example, if a client says there may not be enough resources to respond to an unanticipated request, a short restatement might be, "You are tapped out right now."

In your own words: The surest way to sound inauthentic is to parrot back, word for word, what you hear. For instance, your boss says: "We need to look at the bigger picture," and you reply, "Our eyes should be on the bigger picture." Instead, find your own words that reflect the meaning back to the person. In this instance, a restatement might be, "We are hyper-focused on today's orders when we should be thinking about the macroeconomics in the region."

Not too often: If you interrupt a person to restate, they will get the hint and stop talking. You want them to share their point fully. Wait for a natural pause before offering your understanding. If they don't stop talking and you don't find a natural pause, create one. No one is usually offended if you interrupt to validate what you are hearing. Match their pace and energy, and say, "Hold on. I want to make sure I'm catching it all. There are three issues here: first — ."

The essence: The most effective restatements include the bottom line or heart of what a person is telling you. Especially in groups, people will protect themselves and their ideas if they don't feel as if they are being heard.

Include feelings (when they are a part of the speaker's message): Sometimes, people just want an acknowledgment of how they are feeling, especially when the topic or situation is personal, sensitive, or inflamed. Verbalizing your awareness of their emotions demonstrates deep listening and empathy.

Generally, it is best to simply accept what people say first and check that you understood them correctly before responding with your point of view. Restating demonstrates acceptance — of the fact of their experience — without indicating agreement or disagreement. Defensiveness and listening are inversely related.

Sometimes we might feel that if we truly seek to understand others, we may be signaling agreement, but restating is simply expressing an understanding of another person's point of view. It's not an agreement.

For instance, imagine there is a conflict happening between two members of Sumit's team, and his peer, Li, wants to talk about it with him.

Li (in a hesitant voice): "Can I talk to you about this situation between Alice and Julian? They're on your team, so I realize it is up to you how to handle their personality clash. But people are starting to take sides and they are spending way too much time listening to those two complain about each other. It's affecting how much work is getting done."

Sumit feels a pang of defensiveness. He senses his heart beating faster and his face flushing. His first thought is, *Who are you to tell me what is wrong with my team when you are not perfect, either?* He manages the voice in his head, takes a deep breath, and repeats to himself, *Keep listening.*

Sumit: "Their clash is negatively affecting others."

Li: "Yes. To be honest, I do not think this situation is going to take care of itself. I'm spending a lot of time on damage control with my team. I do not think you have done enough to help these two work out their differences, and I am starting to get frustrated."

Sumit reminds himself that restating isn't agreement, it is just expressing understanding, so he restates Li's point of view.

Sumit: "You think I am part of the problem."

Li: "Well, kind of."

Sumit hears Li confirm his understanding, indicating he was tracking with Li's point of view. Now he can guide the conversation in any number of directions. He can be silent, to allow Li to continue sharing her thoughts and feelings, ask a follow-up question, or share his opposing point of view. Since he does not agree with Li's take on the situation, he expresses this.

Sumit: "I see it differently. I do not think it's a personality clash as much as mixed signals on roles and responsibilities because of the recent department changes. That confusion is causing the flare-ups. I think the way to solve the problem is …"

The conversation continues and Sumit balances listening with talking. The air gets cleared and they work toward a solution. It can be hard to give feedback to a peer, and Li most likely appreciates Sumit being willing to listen to her. Li is more likely to share more information with Sumit knowing he is an astute listener.

Sometimes we miss the signals that tell us it is time to restate. If you are in a conversation with someone and they sound like a broken record, repeating their point over and over, recognize it as a sign that they don't think you heard their point. Saying "I understand" isn't a restatement. Instead, verbalize your understanding.

RESTATE	
How to:	**When to:**
State your understanding of what the other person has said: • Short • In your own words • Just the essence • Not too often • Include emotions *(if it's part of their message)*	• Building rapport • Identifying intentions, values, and emotions • Engaging in a difficult or sensitive conversation • Clarifying a question or objection before responding

---

Try This: Restate

Write down three situations where you want to use listening to avoid miscommunication and/or build better relationships (examples: team meetings, responding to client problems, forming a new relationship).

In one of those upcoming situations, pick one person (a colleague, a client, a friend) and spend five minutes listening to them talk without interrupting. Notice their nonverbal behaviors, look for a moment to restate, and ask curiosity-based questions.

By now, you are getting the hang of listening and that it's not a passive endeavor; that it requires the right mindset and ability to delve below the surface. The last question we'll ponder is next, and we'll offer more skills to further strengthen your listening muscles.

How Am I Listening?

"I don't get it. I have an open-door policy. I don't bite," a frustrated team leader said to Therese. He received low employee engagement scores with feedback that he was intimidating and closed off.

When Therese observed him facilitate a few of his team meetings, she noticed he would interrupt people mid-sentence or offer a skeptical retort. He was unaware that he was listening like a foe, telegraphing his thinking ("That won't work." "I know more about this than you do." "You're wrong.") through his behaviors, and predictably, people shared very little with him because they felt shut down by him.

Contrast that to a conversation with someone listening as a friend. The self-talk they transmit is *I care about what you have to say. Even if I don't like what I'm hearing, I'll keep listening.* It's no surprise that people reveal more to those who listen as a friend because it's like a safe harbor for true dialogue.

Watch those who listen as a friend and you will see three behaviors they consistently do well:

 Send listening signals.

 Draw people out with questions.

 Pause. Create space for people to talk.

Send Listening Signals

In a virtual meeting, Bill appeared stoic and frequently looked down and away from the screen while others talked. His facial expression barely changed, and he stayed silent. When they broke into smaller breakout rooms, he was much more engaged. He summarized the points from earlier and contributed to the conversation.

A colleague remarked, "Wow, Bill, I didn't know you were paying attention this whole time!"

Bill replied with surprise. "Really? I was listening and taking notes." In Bill's mind, he was actively listening, but his body language (no eye contact, looking down, no verbal acknowledgment, no change in facial expression) gave a different impression.

We send silent messages about ourselves as listeners and we're often unaware of the signals we are sending. When words and body language don't match, people tend to believe body language over words.[48] There's a range of nonverbal signals that demonstrates listening — nodding, shifting facial expressions, and eye contact. Those signals encourage the speaker to open up and go deeper.

As humans, we need physical and verbal listening indicators to continue talking. Research reflects that attentive listeners get more insight, information, and relevant details from speakers compared to distracted listeners, even in the absence of asking questions.[49]

A more active indicator of listening is verbal signals. We call them the grunts and groans of good listening. They are sounds and small phrases of encouragement signaling a person to continue talking, like, "Say more." "Wow." "Mm-hmm." "Really?"

The need for those verbal indicators is important in virtual interactions. Eva was talking during a video call and abruptly stopped mid-sentence, wondering aloud, "Did the connection just drop? Are you there?" Because everyone was silent, she thought the screen froze and there was a technical glitch. Several people came off mute to assure her they were listening. In the absence of physical or verbal signals, people stop talking.

These behaviors are almost unconscious skills — and yet, they can quickly establish openness, trust, and respect. We tend to do it when we're interested or we really care about the person speaking to us, but there are times

---

48 Wertheim, E. G. (2008). *The Importance of Effective Communication. Northeastern University.*
49 Pasupathi. M., and Billitteri, J. (2015). Being and Becoming through Being Heard: Listener Effects on Stories and Selves, *International Journal of Listening* 29:2, 67–84, doi: 10.1080/10904018.2015.1029363.

when it's important to listen and we may not have those triggers to listen well. Consciously using these skills will help you and the other person get the communication wheels turning. Bottom line: If you expect to use these skills "automatically" when they're needed, you're probably only half right.

Draw People Out with Questions

Our clients tell us that one of their biggest challenges is simply getting people to speak at all. It's easy to misinterpret silence as meaning that people just are not talkative, aren't interested, or do not have any questions. We are often quick to blame others for the silence, but it is rarely their fault.

Every conversation can be an adventure, an edge-of-your-seat moment when you develop the skill of asking questions. The root of great questions is persistent curiosity — being interested in finding the edges of your knowledge and then expanding it.

Before you pose a question, think about why you are asking it. Your motivation might be to:

Confirm Knowledge: Is what I know valid and complete?

Gather new insights and information: What don't I know? What are people thinking or feeling?

Gain contextual clues: Are my assumptions accurate?

Questions starting with the words *Is, Can*, or *Who* often result in simple yes/no responses. For example, "Is this number final?" (No) or "Can you relate to that problem?" (Yes). These types of closed-ended questions work when your goal is to get specific information quickly or to tie down and validate something. However, they don't give you the information *you don't know you are looking for*.

Open-ended questions often begin with *What, Where, How,* and *Why* and prompt a fuller answer. They tend to kickstart a conversation because it encourages the responder to think versus simply answer. It engages them more. For instance, phrasing a question like, "What do you see as the pros or cons of this idea?" might get a more thoughtful and complete response than, "Can you see how there are upsides and downsides?"

The one question that rarely works at creating engagement is "Any questions?" Think about the last time you heard it. Our guess is that no one replied and yet, it is the most common question people usually ask. Here is why it doesn't work:

 It's too broad. Any questions *about what* exactly? It's hard to answer, so people do not engage.

 It's not expressing genuine interest. It is perfunctory, usually asked at the end of a presentation or meeting when time is running out and does not convey real curiosity.

 It doesn't require people to think. If nothing comes to mind, people will stay silent.

We often invent questions in our minds as we go along. We wing it and miss an opportunity. The next time you are preparing to meet with someone you wish to influence or impress, try to find out everything you can before the conversation. The more you know, the more you can learn. If you know more about their context, they will be more open to engaging with you because you have higher credibility. Your questions will be better and you won't be wasting time asking superficial things.

Ask Targeted Questions	
How to:	**When to:**
Ask open questions when curious. How? _____ What?_____ Describe ... Tell me about ... Ask closed questions to confirm. Is? Did? Will? Can?	The way a question is phrased prompts a certain type of answer. Open questions invite people to give broader answers. Closed questions focus responses. • Use open questions in a conversation to prompt sharing and gather the most information. • Use closed questions to draw out specific information, clarify understanding, or confirm a hunch

Make It Easier to Answer Questions

When we are asked a question, our natural human response is to try to make meaning out of it. We guess about why the person is asking the question — consciously or unconsciously.

Imagine getting a text from your boss that simply says, "Do you have a minute?" You immediately theorize what it is about: "I'm in trouble." "This must be about that email I sent." "They are announcing a change." "It's probably just nothing."

It is easy to assume others know why we are asking a question, and we are often wrong. That lack of context can result in misunderstandings, and the quality, accuracy, and completeness of their answers are degraded.

Picture a team meeting where the leader asks, "Why is it taking so long to get this done?" Everyone starts mentally guessing why they asked the question. One person thinks, *She thinks we aren't doing a good job.* Another thinks, *She must want the details about what we're doing.* Another thinks, *Our sales territory is more complex than others. She doesn't get it.*

Their guesses influence how they respond to the question. They may get defensive, shade the truth, give more information than needed, or give the wrong information. There are more hurdles to getting real information. When people apply their own filters to questions, it makes it more likely to not find out what really is going on.

The antidote to avoiding misunderstanding, getting quicker answers, and eliciting more replies is to preview the question. To preview simply means telling people why you're asking a question, or at least what you'll do with the answer (preferably something beneficial to those who respond). It helps people respond more directly (because they know what you need and why) and more honestly (because they generally feel more comfortable with the context). It creates an atmosphere where real information is likely to flow.

For instance, here are different previews to the same question. Note how the answers might change depending on the context.

"Why is it taking so long?"

 "I'm not blaming anyone. I want to use our situation to troubleshoot the process. Why is it taking so long?"

 "Last month, you said you were on track to finish. Why is it taking so long?"

 "In all regions, we are struggling with getting customers on board. Why is it taking so long"?

A preview helps define the question in a way that takes the guesswork out of the exchange and makes it easier for people to reply. Being direct with questions this way gives credibility to the questioner and confidence to the responder because they know what they are looking for. Previewing is a way to create safety and lower risk. For instance, when people sense you're looking for a right/wrong answer, they won't speak up for fear of making a mistake. Previewing can lower feelings of risk.

We think it is always a good idea to preview questions, and it's especially true in these situations:

 A new relationship where you're learning each other's communication styles

 Power dynamics at play where people can jump to (wrong) conclusions

 Working with people at a distance or where language barriers exist

When looking for fast answers; context helps someone zero in on what you want

 Low trust relationships where misunderstandings persist

Try This: Preview a Question

Prepare a preview for a question that makes it more likely you will get open and honest responses. Remember: A preview is simply giving context, stating why you're asking the question or what you plan to do with the answer.

Example: **Do you have a minute?**

Preview #1: The new managing director wants to meet you. Do you have a minute?

Preview #2: We're about to finalize next year's budget and I want to run a number by you. Do you have a minute?

Preview #3: Something hilarious just happened. Do you have a minute?

Your Question:

_____

_____

_____

Your preview to the question:

_____

_____

_____

- -

Preview Questions	
How to:	**When to:**
State why you are asking the question or how you will use the answer.	• Learning the complete picture of a situation • Repeating a question to get a more complete answer • Shifting the flow or direction of a conversation • Handling objections

Pause — Create Space

As useful as questions can be, a whole series of them without listening and making space for answers becomes an interrogation. Asking questions gives us a sense of control in the conversation, but pausing is real control. Rapid-fire questions without a break tend to put people on the defensive. Instead, stay silent for a few seconds — even ten seconds after asking a question. We know that might feel like a lifetime, but thoughtful, curious questions require people to slow down and think. A pause provides the moment to consider and then respond.[50]

When you stay silent, you create the space for the person to share even more. The silence allows the person to catch

50 Curhan, J.R., Overbeck, J.R., Cho, Y., Zhang, T., and Yang, Y. 2021. Silence is golden: extended silence, deliberative mindset, and value creation in negotiation. *J. Appl. Psychol.*

up with their own thinking and get comfortable sharing more layers of information. People are often testing your interest level: "Do you really want to hear this? Are you actually listening?" Pausing, in combination with nonverbal listening signals (eye contact, remaining silent, mirroring their expression), validates their impression that you're genuinely interested.

Do not give up on a question if it does not get an immediate response. We often see people jumping from question to question before the responder can get their answer started. It may sound something like, "What is your budget for this project?" [no pause] "How are you allocating your resources?" [no pause] "Is senior leadership serious about their investment in this project?" Stacking questions or asking multiple questions all at once is confusing and is likely to lead to the responder picking and choosing what they want to share. As a result, the questioner gets limited information. Ask one question at a time, followed by a pause, to get more complete answers.

If it is hard to pause after asking a question, remind yourself that silence may be a good thing. People need time to reflect before responding. Notice how long your partner pauses between sentences, and in the course of the conversation, try to match that length. It is an effective way to gauge what will feel comfortable versus awkward when it comes to pausing.[51]

51 University of Gothenburg (2015, Sept 30). Pauses Can Make or Break a Conversation. ScienceDaily. Retrieved January 16, 2023, from www.sciencedaily.com/releases/2015/09/150930110555.htm

Get People to Talk	
Less of	**More of**
• Ask multiple questions without a pause. • Ask questions without listening to the answers. • Answer your own questions. • Rely on a few people to answer every question. • State assumptions versus test assumptions: "I'm sure we all agree that ..."	• Pause. • Look at people when they talk. • Use short sounds to demonstrate you're listening: "Oh," "Mm-hmm." • Invite individual perspectives. Ask questions that build on earlier answers. • Create space for those who need it. "Let's hear from people who haven't had a chance to speak yet."

Focusing on the three questions of Who am I listening to? What am I listening for? and How am I listening? enables people to catapult their facilitation capability. It's why we often call it the Clark Kent of facilitation skills: This technique might be often underestimated, but can reveal itself to have great superpowers, just like Superman.

Chapter Takeaways

- Being a great listener requires attention, focus, and letting go of control. It accelerates connection, influence, respect, and problem-solving.

- To advance your listening skills, consider:

  - Who am I listening to? Recognize who or what gets your attention and its impact on your ability to listen.

  - What am I listening for? Don't take words at face value; explore deeper nuances to understand the real message.

- How am I listening? Choose to listen as a friend (vs. a foe), being open, curious, and interested.

- Restating what someone says is a straightforward way to ensure that both of you are on the same page. It establishes trust and credibility by accurately capturing the speaker's message or emotions in your own words.

- The root of great questions is persistent curiosity — being interested in finding the edges of your knowledge and then expanding it.

- Make it easier for others to answer questions by offering the context (a preview) for why you are asking the question.

- Balance talking with pauses to encourage others to say more.

9 Serve the Purpose

Balance keeping on track with adapting for impact.

I clarify the purpose and goals to provide focus and direction.

When the group goes off track, I redirect them to bring the focus back to the purpose and goal.

I adjust when the process is no longer serving the group or the desired outcome.

I manage unexpected challenges and events with grace and calm.

Of all the contributions, this chapter might be the one people most associate with facilitation. Ultimately, knowing your goals and then making choices to serve them lies at the very heart of everything we have offered so far. Similar to a jazz band leader, this contribution requires the facilitator to listen, keep tempo, play their part, riff off what others do, and improvise. It involves surfing the tension between focused planning and responding to needs in the moment. Truly serving the purpose of an event means navigating and negotiating many, often conflicting factors.

Balance Planning and Presence

Good conversations aren't always linear, and side trips that seem like detours at first may actually add value. Knowing when to intervene or allow for an off-roading conversation is both art and science.

There's a natural tension between sticking to the agenda and flexing to the needs of the group. Sometimes, there are competing goals and values to negotiate. Even when the agenda is agreed upon, people with influence may work in opposition to them, making forward progress difficult. A stray comment can trigger emotions or tangential thoughts, and just like that, the group is offtrack.

How do we balance keeping on track with adapting to the needs and wants of the group? How do we juggle one person's interests and needs with others? How do power dynamics affect our choices? What about our own goals in light of the goals of others?

Consider this scenario: Sam is meeting with the chief human resource officer and the director of talent management to develop leadership expectations for their growing company. While the meeting request is unexpected, Sam is happy to see one of the business leaders in attendance. Shortly into the conversation, the business leader interrupts and says, "Creating leadership competencies is nice to do, but we don't have time. We're facing high turnover because of poor people leadership. We need to be talking about training."

What would you do if you were in Sam's shoes?

Follow the business leader's path in the conversation.

 Invite the group to decide — "Here's what we planned to discuss, but training is also an important issue. How would we like to spend our time?"

 Redirect the conversation — "That's not what we're here to talk about. Let's schedule a different meeting to talk about training."

 Do something else.

You could make a case for any of these choices.

When you're faced with options, such as stick to the agenda or go off-roading, a question we often ask ourselves is: What's in the best service of the group right now? Do people need to work through a team-related issue before they can work on a task? Sometimes, that answer is to take the detour and other times, it's to stay the course.

Succeeding at this endeavor begins before you ever enter the room and continues after your event is over. Let's break it down.

Keep-on-Track Considerations	
Stick to the Path	**Take the Detour**
There's a tight timeline or deadline.	There's an elephant in the room: People are carefully selecting their words, not participating, or shifting uncomfortably.
What's in and out of scope has been clearly defined and agreed upon by the participants.	Participants continue to express an underlying issue that has to be resolved first.
There's another outlet for items that can't be addressed or resolved in the meeting.	There's consensus to focus on a different topic.

Before an Engagement

Let's be real: Plenty of times, when invited to attend a meeting or schedule a conversation, we find ourselves thinking, *Why are we meeting?* and *Couldn't this just be an email?* Without context and a clear purpose, it's easy to be pessimistic or even defensive before the event starts. Therese once received a calendar invite from a colleague that read, *"Update (I'll tell you why we're meeting when we talk)."* She wasted hours wondering and worrying about what the meeting could be about, even dragging in two of her colleagues to solicit their theories on this big mystery. What a waste!

It's easy to assume that everyone knows the meeting purpose or that things will just fall into place, especially with recurring meetings or with colleagues we know. But the truth is, preparation is the first essential step for any gathering, whether it's recurring or not.

Clarify the Purpose and Goal

Start by identifying your purpose and goals. Defining the purpose — the core why of a gathering — is like setting your compass for a chosen destination. A clear and agreed-upon purpose allows you to pinpoint specific outcomes and goals that arise naturally from that purpose. Goals address the question of What should be discovered, accomplished, or produced at this moment?

Sylvia was a solution architect at her software company responsible for leading multi-day implementation workshops with new clients. The workshops were designed to gather requirements, uncover client constraints, and build the implementation plan. When she tried to schedule it with clients, she usually got some pushback about the meeting length ("Can't we just do this in a couple of hours?") and they would balk at the number of people expected to attend. After running into that resistance enough times, she knew she had to make a more compelling case for the workshop. In her pre-planning client calls, she gained buy-in faster by offering the purpose and goal like this:

Purpose — "The workshop purpose is to ease the transition into using the new platform and ensure it's designed and implemented most effectively."

Goal — "We have three goals. First, it's to identify areas for customization to enhance the user experience and align with your customer-first values. The second goal is to accelerate the team's readiness and buy-in by providing hands-on experience and getting their feedback. And finally, we'll build the integration plan together to minimize disrupting the flow of business and meet your timelines."

Define the Type of Meeting Goals

Meetings tend to fall into three categories: informational, problem-solving, and relationship-building. Each meeting type requires specific planning in terms of agenda, time, and resources. Identifying the goal streamlines the planning process, ensuring the meeting is structured to achieve the desired results.

When participants know the meeting goals in advance, they can prepare mentally and come ready with relevant information, ideas, or questions. Having context for the meeting promotes active engagement and participation, whether it's actively listening during an informational meeting, problem-solving collaboratively, or fostering open communication in a relationship-building meeting, so participants can contribute meaningfully when they know the type of meeting they are attending.

Goal/Meeting Type	How to Start on Track
Informational Communicating news or updates to ensure everyone knows simultaneously	• Communicate the reason/importance and why it's best shared live. • Provide pre-reading and what attendees are expected to bring (such as status updates, examples, feedback).
Problem-Solving Collaborating to reach solutions to complex problems	• Define the problem (don't assume everyone sees it the same way). • Clarify the decision-making process. • Identify what is in and out of scope.
Relationship-Building Creating connection and fostering camaraderie	• Consider what people already know about each other. • Plan for what people need to feel safe with one another.

In Sylvia's software integration workshop, the meeting was a blend of informational and problem-solving. She would start with teaching people about the platform's features and functionality. Then she'd transition to decision-making discussions, allowing users to address challenges and make customization decisions, clarifying for both her and participants.

Determine the Attendees

"Make purpose your bouncer," writes Priya Parker in *The Art of Gathering*[52]. A well-defined meeting purpose enables you to discern who should attend. Sometimes, we over-include people because we don't want to offend anyone and deal with the consequences. And sometimes the invitation list swells because of the culture. We've worked with some companies that highly

---

52 Parker, P. (2018). *The Art of Gathering: How We Meet and Why It Matters*. Riverhead Books.

value collaboration, which gets misinterpreted because everyone has to be included. People who won't fulfill the purpose detract from it, diluting focus and engagement, and hindering progress.

Informational	Problem-Solving	Team Alignment Relationship-Building
• Who needs to hear it? • Who will be directly affected by it? • Who will need to act quickly on it?	• Who is directly involved? • Who is affected by decisions? • Who has valuable perspective or expertise to bring?	• Who needs to feel like they belong? • What level of team cohesion is critical to your purpose?

Every person affects the dynamics of a group, so consider each person's role, expertise, and contribution.

In Sylvia's pre-planning call, she encouraged her client to limit the number of participants to the primary users, key decision-makers, and those who had the most influence in making the change happen. Doing so made the most of everyone's time and expertise, resulting in faster decision-making and buy-in.

The questions above should help you determine who should attend. Use the following chart to help with your final participant list.

Who Should Attend the Meeting?		
ESSENTIAL *(Key Stakeholders, Subject Matter Experts, Decision-Makers)*	**OPTIONAL** *(Input is beneficial but not required)*	**INFORMED** *(Made aware but do not participate)*
• Contributes expertise and insights relevant to the meeting topic. • Holds authority to make decisions and drive outcomes. • Takes action on meeting outcomes	• Provides knowledge or input to enhance the process but absence won't hinder progress. • May hold some influence but are not critical for final decisions.	• Kept in the loop. • Awareness of meeting outcomes helps ensure transparency and alignment within the team.

Defining the purpose, goals, meeting types, and attendees will put you a long way toward ensuring an effective and fulfilling event. Answer these questions before diving into a specific flow or process.

Clarify Roles and Responsibilities

When we coach people who want to develop more skills at keeping on track, we often hear concerns that revolve around the roles and responsibilities in the meeting. For instance,

 "The client will perceive me as rude if I interrupt them to stay on track."

 "When the VP is in the room, I feel like I need to defer to her instead of taking command of the meeting."

 "My co-facilitator might feel like I'm taking over if I speak up during their segment."

Those moments of uncertainty or hesitation can be avoided by making clear agreements about roles and responsibilities in this planning stage. Standard meeting roles include:

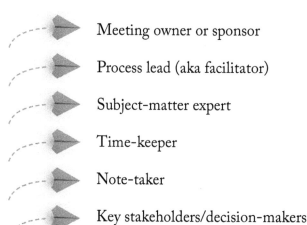

Meeting owner or sponsor

Process lead (aka facilitator)

Subject-matter expert

Time-keeper

Note-taker

Key stakeholders/decision-makers

Can one person play more than one role? Yes. Meeting owners often facilitate their own meetings, although there are situations when it's best to step back from the facilitator role to allow themselves to participate more meaningfully.

Realistically, when facilitating internally, a process lead may also have subject-matter expertise or a stake in decisions. In a situation like this, it helps to let people know transparently what role you're playing from moment to moment. That might sound like, "I'm taking my facilitator hat off for a moment. I'd like to add my point of view here."

Getting on the same page regarding roles at this planning stage focuses you and your participants. Then, collectively, you can truly serve your purpose.

Try This: Prepare for an Upcoming Meeting

Purpose • What problem, challenge, or opportunity will it address? • How will it contribute to the overall objectives of the project, team, or organization?	
Goals • What are the specific outcomes or deliverables? • How will we measure the effectiveness of the meeting?	
Meeting Type • Is the main priority to inform, solve, or build relationships? • In what ways will the meeting type inform the format? (e.g., if the meeting type is to build relationships, should it be in-person or virtual?)	
Who's Invited • What roles or expertise are necessary to achieve the meeting goals? • Who is essential to contribute to the discussion or decision-making? • Who is directly involved or affected by the meeting's purpose and goals?	

Design the Agenda

In the same way that your meeting purpose sets your compass, an agenda acts as your road map: It provides a clear path and direction, ensuring everyone stays focused on the purpose and goals.

An effective agenda is designed around the meeting purpose and type. For instance, if it's an information-sharing meeting, consider presentations, Q&A sessions, or knowledge-sharing exercises. For problem-solving meetings, include activities like brainstorming, analyzing options, and decision-making. For relationship-building meetings, incorporate open discussions and activities that enable people to get to know each other better.

Informational	Problem-Solving	Relationship-Building
• Use visual aids such as slides, charts, or diagrams to enhance. understanding and retention • Establish the order in which information should be shared. • Prepare stories and examples. • Build in time for Q&A. • Incorporate interactive elements such as group discussions, polls, or brief activities to encourage active involvement.	• Allocate time for brainstorming to generate ideas. • Use decision-making tools and techniques (pros and cons lists, voting, etc.). • Allocate time to develop an action plan with responsibilities and timelines.	• Incorporate activities to help. participants connect and build rapport. • Carve out time for open and honest discussions about team dynamics, strengths, challenges, and areas for improvement.

Try This: Draft an Agenda

Draft an agenda that supports your goals and objectives. (See "Share Subject-Matter Knowledge" and "Suit the Context" chapters for key questions to help you plan your flow.)

During the Meeting

Establish Ground Rules

The facilitator's job is to create an environment that supports the purpose of the meeting or event. The starting point is often ground rules. It's akin to the lines on a sports field. Just as those lines define the boundaries and rules of the game, ground rules set the parameters and expectations for how the group will interact. They ensure everyone knows how to engage, promoting fair play and a level playing field for communication and collaboration.

When offering ground rules to a group, treat the process as a conversation, not an expectation. It's easy to misinterpret people's silence as agreement when in reality, it may feel too risky to disagree with a ground rule. For example, "Let's all be open, honest, and candid" might be too much of a stretch for a group with mistrust and strong power dynamics. If there is not already trust, who will speak up to challenge that ground rule?

Balancing setting parameters yourself and sourcing agreements from the group takes finesse. Some of you will want to introduce and advocate for yourself because of your experience, values, and expertise. For example, a standard ground rule that many groups will offer up is "Assume positive intent." That sounds great on the surface, but as equity and inclusion professionals know, assuming positive intent is only half of an equation that will support belonging and courageous communication. The other half requires us to take accountability for our actions and words.

We must recognize that regardless of our intentions, we might hurt or offended others. When that happens, a safe collaborative space allows for the affected person to speak up. Rather than only including "Assume positive intent," we now offer ground rules that address both assumptions and impact.

When the meeting is intended to drive engagement, interaction, and inclusivity, here are some of our go-to approaches:

Ground Rules to Promote Engagement and Inclusivity	
Curiosity	Curiosity is the fuel for growth. If your mind wanders to *I already know this* or *They are wrong,* we will shift our mindset to curiosity. For instance, *I wonder how that might work?* or *What assumptions am I making?*
Consideration	We agree to listen and be open to other points of view. We will support each other in being vulnerable, speaking our truth, and trying new things. We will take accountability for our impact, as well as assuming positive intent.
Commitment	This is tied to consideration. Everyone's time is valuable. Getting the most out of that time requires commitment. When the meeting is in session, we agree to be here physically and mentally.
Confidentiality	Anything said here — about people, issues, or the organization — stays with us. We agree to share our personal learnings, but any stories, examples, or private information will be kept confidential.
Contribute as much as you consume	The best experiences are ones where we learn from each other. It's everyone's job to offer insights, ideas, and questions as much as it is to learn.

As important as it may be to offer ground rules, invite and welcome pushback on them. By inviting everyone into the process, you create a sense of ownership and investment. The more the group is involved in defining these behavioral agreements, the more likely members are to adhere to them. We first learned about the importance of adding words about impact to our positive intent ground rule when participants in a workshop pointed it out. In a more straightforward way, some groups will be very open to putting away their electronic devices. Others don't find this feasible. It's better to know up front than to set a ground rule that won't be honored.

Treating ground rules as a collaborative effort gives you license to hold people accountable. Petra tried this approach in her monthly cross-functional team meeting. The group agreed to the ground rules (everyone participates, no talking over one another, and parking lot for off-topic items). At one point, it felt like pulling teeth to get people to speak up. She remembered the group agreement and that gave her the confidence to mention it.

She said, "I'm noticing a lot of silence, although you all agreed you would participate. What's holding you back?" Someone hesitantly spoke up and offered concern about the feasibility of the timeline. Reminding people of the group agreement can be a nonthreatening way to keep things on track and identify when something needs addressing, even if it was not in the plan.

Monitor Focus and Purpose

Once the meeting starts, don't assume that your plan will simply magically unfold. To paraphrase President Dwight D. Eisenhower, "Planning is imperative; the plan is useless." Watch for early signals of confusion or lack of motivation. Are people asking questions not relevant to the topic? Who is talking and not talking? Are people shifting nervously in their seats?

The best way to check in is to ask open questions that encourage people to reflect about what's happening. Even when all signs point to things going smoothly, it's still wise to ask the group, especially if it's a new group or process.

Questions for Monitoring the Track
"It seems like the group's energy and engagement took a dip when we moved to this topic. How should we interpret that?"
"Let's pause for a check-in. How is this process working for everyone?"
"I'm noticing some confused expressions right now. What's unclear?"
"We've had a few people giving most of the input so far. Who hasn't weighed in yet?"
"It's taken us about fifteen minutes to reach a decision about our first of three topics. We have one hour remaining. Is this method still working for everyone?"
"Does anybody need to find out anything else before we move on?"
"I'm noticing more people ducking in and out of the meeting. Is now a good time for a break?"

Don't overlook the signs that indicate you, the leader/facilitator, are unclear. Imagine moments when the group is talking about something you don't know about or you don't understand, or you're having difficulty making connections with what you're hearing. Tune into your emotions. Are you nervous, frustrated, anxious? Then notice what you're saying to yourself. If your self-talk is *I'm lost and I'm supposed to be in charge*, it's likely to lead to feelings of panic and insecurity. If we could plant a different seed of self-talk in your mind, it would be this: *I'm not following what's happening, but I know what to do to get in sync.*

Here's how to manage the moment:

 Be observant. Are others confused or on track? If it's only you who is confused, let the conversation continue for a few more minutes.

 Listen deeply to get in sync with the group.

If others appear confused, pause and ask a question for clarity. If you're not clear, there's a good chance that others aren't, either.

Get Back on Track

When things go off the rails, sometimes the meeting design is the source of that confusion — maybe a section of the agenda doesn't work and sometimes that is facilitator error, meaning you didn't give adequate guidance.

We can get easily triggered by people's behaviors — someone talks too much or no one talks, people join late or multitask, someone derails the conversation. In those moments when you feel your blood pressure rise, take a step back and get curious. Ask yourself, *What might be driving their behavior?* Sometimes there's an underlying reason that, if addressed, will get things back on track. When you facilitate from a place of empathy versus frustration and judgment, you are more equipped to manage the moment in a productive way.

What's Happening	What Might Be Under the Surface
A person derails the meeting with a lot of questions. "Why are we doing this?" "I thought we were meeting about something else."	They feel in the dark because they were left out of earlier conversations and resent being included so late in the process/project.
The primary decision-maker interrupts you and says, "Can you just hit the highlights?"	They want to know the bottom line as quickly as possible.
A participant holds a side conversation with another person. They appear to ignore you.	They think you and others will not be open to hearing their point of view, so they share it with someone whom they feel is safe.
Someone asks off-topic questions.	They have some good ideas somewhat related to the meeting, but rarely have a chance to share them with this group. It's important to have their ideas heard and acknowledged.

Pause and Reset

If people are off-track, stop what you are doing (and what they are doing). It's akin to pulling over to the side of the road. Say what you see — describe the behaviors you've observed that indicate the group is off-track — and invite the group to share more about what's happening and what would help them get back on track. Often, simply reminding people of the objective or where you are in the meeting is all they need to redirect themselves. Sometimes, though, you may need to stop and explore the situation with curiosity.

Call Out Patterns

Leaders hold the space for people by being fully present and listening to what's being said and what's not being said. When groups appear to spin their wheels, one of the best ways to get back on track is to listen intently to what's causing the lack of forward progress and then name it for the benefit of the group.

In the "Listen" chapter, we offer the skill of restating to verbalize your understanding of a person's or group's point of view. Restating to a group requires your full attention to notice patterns of behavior. We strongly suggest reading that chapter because the listening skill turbo-charges your ability to spot and call out patterns in a way that won't put people on the defensive. When people feel acknowledged and understood, they tend to be more open to moving forward.

Identify and Call Out Patterns	
The Behavior	**How to Address It**
People use jargon, acronyms, or clichés.	"We're using a lot of acronyms. I'm not sure those newer to the team understand. Can you clarify?"
Multiple people make the same point (using slightly different words) and don't realize it.	"It seems like we're all in agreement. We're saying we need to renegotiate the vendor contract before the year's end."
The discussion is focused on the symptoms and not the root cause.	"I'm noticing the focus is on what you dislike about the template and not how we can make the pricing formula simpler. If we focus on pricing first, it might resolve some of the template issues."
The group gets stuck on one topic.	"We all have ideas about how to fix the problem and Fin has agreed to be the point person. Instead of troubleshooting now, send your ideas to him after the meeting. Can you all agree to that? [*After affirmative responses*] Great — let's move on."
The group isn't listening to one another.	"Terry, I'm not sure you understood Cara's point. Cara, please say that one more time."
Group tension is shutting down the conversation.	"It's clear everyone wants the same outcome: to do what's best for the students, given the limited resources. The comments are getting personal, which is taking the focus away from the problem."
Only a few are speaking.	"So far, the majority of the input has come from the people who have been here the longest. Let's hear from those who are newer to the team."
Someone is interrupting.	"Bianca, excuse me. Mary was explaining her situation when you offered your perspective. Let Mary finish and then the floor is yours."
People sidetrack the conversation.	"Let's take a pause. We've spent fifteen minutes talking about the warehouse problem in the eastern region, but it's not an issue elsewhere. We're trying to solve the problem across all regions."
The group is going into more-than-necessary details.	"We're only about halfway through and we're aiming to be done by noon. To move faster, let's summarize rather than going into lots of detail."

Manage Time

You look up at the clock and wonder what happened to the time — you are forty-five minutes behind schedule and there's no way to meet the objectives at the current pace. What do you do?

 Hit the fast-forward button and sprint to the end?

 Drop a whole agenda topic and hope no one notices?

 Tell everyone that they will have to stay an extra forty-five minutes?

You have choices in those moments, and the best choice is the one that serves the group and its objectives. Less-disruptive options include controlling the length of the conversation with simple phrases like "One final comment" or "We're moving on after we hear one more point of view." That's an effective and respectful way to proactively manage time.

When you're really behind on time, you need a bigger intervention. Look first at ways to shorten breaks without zapping people's energy. Another option is getting an agreement that you'll end the session later than scheduled.

If those aren't realistic choices, try giving a briefer overview, assigning independent work, or shortening discussions/activities.

Reach Agreement on Actions and Next Steps

The last minutes of a meeting are often like the final mile on a long run: People are mentally fatigued, distracted, and ready to be done, yet that's when you need everyone's attention and commitment for the next steps. Now is the time to agree upon and confirm decisions, action items, owners, and timelines. To keep on track, either summarize or have the group summarize those agreed-upon elements.

One of the gifts you can offer in those final moments is a reality check on action items and the next steps. A surefire way for things to go off track after the meeting is when people over-commit to actions or timelines. An effective screen for action is the F.I.T. filter, which comes from Erika Andersen's book, *Being Strategic.*[53] F.I.T. is an acronym for feasible, impactful, and timely. It's an effective way to help a group decide on the actions that will best support them toward their desired outcomes.

Feasibility: Is it possible to accomplish this? Do we have the skills, resources, time, and support to do it? Imagine an overzealous group agreeing to a certain deliverable in one week. You could be a force for good by asking, "Is that really possible? Next week is the end of the quarter and that means half the team will be focused on financials. Do we have the resources?" Then allow the group to discuss and decide.

Impact: Is it the best use of limited resources? Will it give you the biggest bang for the buck? Help the group

---

53 Andersen, E. (2009). *Being Strategic.* St. Martin's Press.

get the maximum value for their actions with the least amount of effort. You might say, "There are a lot of actions on your list, and you still have your day-to-day tasks on top of this. Of all the actions, which ones do you think will move you fastest and most effectively to your goal?"

Timeliness: This means two things; it's about order and opportunity. When you begin to create action plans, there are things you need to start doing right from the beginning. That's order. For instance, a team might need to get funding for the project as a first step. The opportunity refers to circumstances that you can take advantage of. For instance, if the senior team has their monthly meeting next week, a short-term tactic might be to get on their agenda to pitch the idea and make a funding request.

Flex Your Approach

Cross your arms.

Now cross them the other way.

How awkward did that feel? If it took you a few seconds or you're thinking it's the wrong way, congratulations! You just ran into one of your habits. Most habits aren't good or bad; they are just the way we operate.

As we look at how best to "Serve the Purpose," it behooves us to notice our habitual choices and work to expand our range and avoid ruts that are not useful.

We all have our own style when it comes to leading interactions. Your facilitation trademark might be that of an energizer, amping up the fun and engagement, or it might be the empath, holding space for the group by creating a respectful, calm, and serene environment. You might lean into driver behaviors and be known for leading an efficient and direct path to accomplishing the goal.

There is no one best style. Rather, there's a time, place, and purpose for all styles. We've observed thousands of facilitators over the years, and the quality that separates exceptional from average facilitators is their ability to flex out of their preferred style and adapt to the needs of the group when called upon. For example, a facilitator with a more caregiving style can shift to taking command and being decisive when the group loses focus. Another skillful facilitator might prefer efficiency and speed, but flexes to a more casual pace and lighthearted humor as they notice tension building among frustrated colleagues.

Felix, the head of operations, found himself in a pivotal meeting with three members of a small family-run business recently acquired by his employer. Known for his no-nonsense demeanor and straight-to-the-point approach, he wasted no time diving into the balance sheet and bombarding the family members with an array of probing questions. The replies he received were terse and off-topic.

Later, when Felix debriefed with his manager, he admitted that the meeting didn't go well, saying, "It was like pulling teeth. We just didn't click."

At the root of the issue was a clash of styles. His business-like formality, while a great fit for his company culture, clashed with the family's collegial, informal, and relaxed atmosphere. In hindsight, he realized that if he had tried a more adaptable approach and built a relationship with the family first, before getting right to tasks, he would have gotten a lot further.

If we were to coach Felix as he prepares for his next meeting, we'd offer a few questions for adapting his approach to yield better outcomes.

 What are your goals and values?

 What are your audience's values and preferred ways of operating?

 What is your range of options?

These days, we're awash with personality tests like Myers-Briggs, DiSC, CliftonStrengths, and the Color Code. We're also skeptical of categorizing people because humans are not one "thing" and to label people as a personality type is unhelpful at best and dangerous at worst.[54,55]Instead, the focus should be on knowing your style strengths and weaknesses, and developing the capability to make temporary behavioral shifts to align with the group in support of desired outcomes. We're not talking about being manipulative or inauthentic. Instead,

54 Gardner, W. L., and Martinko, M. J. (1996). Using the Myers-Briggs Type Indicator to Study Managers: A Literature Review and Research Agenda. *Journal of Management* 22(1), 45–83. https://doi.org/10.1177/014920639602200103.
55 Hussey I, Hughes S. Hidden Invalidity Among 15 Commonly Used Measures in Social and Personality Psychology. Advances in Methods and Practices in Psychological Science. 2020;3(2):166-184. doi:10.1177/2515245919882903

flexing your approach to the needs of others is an act of service and respect and it builds connection.

For example:

A detail-oriented and methodical leader notices he's losing the group's attention. He shifts by increasing his pace and getting more concise.

A person who prefers to start meetings with personal anecdotes and stories reads the body language of others (a not-so-subtle glance at a watch) and pivots by getting to the task at hand.

A team member who prefers to move quickly through meeting agenda topics slows the pace and shifts to a more conversational approach when they see the group be more engaged and energized by group discussion.

Alona, the head of talent acquisition, needed to train her direct reports on a new talent acquisition process. She went into the meeting thinking, *This will be easy. They are all smart and want this change.* Her habit was to move fast through the details, but she noticed this usually talkative group remaining quiet. "Are there any questions?" she asked. No one spoke up.

Alona paused and said, "Okay. What's going on?" After a moment of uncomfortable silence, the most senior team member asked in a pessimistic tone, "So the hiring managers have to get *all* that documentation to us before we can initiate a search?" Then another chimed in, "Do the business leaders know this?" Followed by a third,

"Yeah, and what happens when they try and work around this new process? They don't respect us. Who's going to hold them accountable?"

Those questions felt like speed bumps to Alona because they interrupted her natural desire to move fast and not get mired in details. She had a choice at that moment. She could continue as planned and take a "Let's cross that bridge when we come to it" approach, move into a problem-solving discussion, or even end the meeting. She decided to build on their offers, which were:

 A concern about organizational buy-in

 A sense of powerlessness in holding the hiring manager accountable

 An awareness of how the new process will require behavioral change

Alona thought, *They aren't being resistant; they are raising valid concerns. They care about talent acquisition as much as I do.*

She replied, "Yes, this means hiring managers need to change, and a more consistent process means we can fill open positions faster. How about we pause on the mechanics and talk about what it will take to change hiring manager behavior?"

With head nods all around, one direct report said, "Yes. The mechanics are the easy part and, frankly, we can learn that on our own. We need to focus on what could get in the way of making this happen."

In this situation, the context was important because there was a power dynamic at play, too. Her team felt disrespected by hiring managers. Alona showed respect by accepting their redirection to tackle hiring manager behavior and save the system mechanics for later.

The more experienced you become, the greater the risk of falling into a routine, letting your guard down, and making assumptions. Let's look at Lora, an experienced consultant, who was leading a meeting with a client team when she noticed the conversation spinning in circles and people talking over one another.

She took command, calling the group to order, and declared a new direction by saying, "Here's how we'll move forward." In Lora's experience, teams typically appreciated her decisiveness and clarity — but not this one.

The group revolted and said, "You can't tell us what to do!" The team leader quickly called a break and approached Lora, saying he didn't appreciate how she took over the meeting. While their group's process was messy, it worked for them and they preferred it, even if it meant it took longer than planned. It was a revelation to Lora that the choice she typically makes wouldn't fit every situation or group.

Try This: Flex Your Approach

How would you describe your facilitation style?

What are situations where your facilitation style is most effective?

When might it be less of a fit for the audience or situation?

Accept the Unexpected

Therese was leading a three-day event with twenty-five leaders when one participant approached her during a break. He raised his shirt sleeve to reveal a nasty red rash that he said had appeared out of nowhere, so he was going to skip out to an urgent care center.

No one was prepared for what happened next.

When he reappeared a few hours later, the concern etched on his face could have launched a thousand panic attacks. His itchy rash was not an innocent annoyance; it was a confirmation of bedbugs at the hotel everyone was staying at. Picture all twenty-four heads spinning around in perfect synchronization, their expressions a mix of horror and dread, as they fixated on Therese and her co-facilitator. The meticulously laid-out agenda and carefully crafted plans? Out the window! What was supposed to be a quick lunch break turned into an unexpected and unplanned three-hour escapade as everyone hustled to secure alternative accommodations.

Ideally, you won't to have to deal with something as strange as that, but there are plenty of other curveballs when working with groups because the unexpected happens all the time. Consider scenarios like these:

- Having to condense your thirty-minute presentation into just ten minutes

- Experiencing a technical glitch in the middle of your presentation

- Realizing your audience isn't fluent in your spoken language

- Having a heated argument erupt during a meeting

Those moments are like turbulence during a flight, prompting passengers to seek out cues for guidance. Should they brace for impact or continue watching their movie? We look to flight attendants because they're adept at managing most situations, whether dealing with disruptive passengers to preparing for extreme turbulence. A group will look to you as the facilitator to lead them.

In the same way, the more you know how to manage the unexpected and unplanned, the more people want to follow your lead. Sometimes the situation requires a bigger shift from you than just a tweak to the agenda. While we can't give you solutions to every possible scenario (who could have predicted bedbugs?), we can offer ways to expand your performance range because the more versatile you are in flexing to the needs of the group while keeping the objectives in clear view, the more positive an impact you make.

Accept Offers

Ultimately, facilitating in this way is improvising, and engaging the "Yes, and" principle, the mother of all improvisational theater tenets, will help you navigate whatever comes up, whether you expected it (or like it) or not.

Improvisers talk about everything they see, hear, and sense as being an offer — a gift from which to create. And offers are all around us. For example:

 The client flips to the last page of your report as you begin to present.

 The decision-maker leans in, smiles, and nods their head in agreement.

 Your manager subtly looks at their watch as you talk.

We naturally accept and build on offers that align with our values and objectives because they resonate with our beliefs and aspirations. For instance, while presenting a new initiative, you notice the participants nodding in agreement and showing genuine interest. Recognizing their receptivity, you build on the offer by telling a story to enhance their understanding.

Conversely, we tend to resist offers that don't fit with our goals, intentions, or values because they may challenge our established beliefs or divert us from our intended path. For example, while discussing a change happening in the department, a team member crosses their arms and rolls their eyes. While noticing it, you don't acknowledge it. When we ignore, shut down, or debate offers, it has a negative impact on our interactions. It diminishes people's willingness to engage, which hinders collaboration and limits our ability to guide groups to their intended destination.

Although many of us these days have heard of the "Yes, and" principle, it's often misunderstood. The term connotes a practice, a way of listening, noticing, and collaborating. Sometimes it may mean, "I agree with your idea, feeling, or premise" — but not always. It simply signals acceptance. In some cultures, yes signals acknowledgment or a sign of respect rather than agreement,[56] which can be confusing to other cultures.

However, "Yes, and" does not imply you have to *like* everything. It simply means that if something exists in the conversation, ignoring or arguing with it won't get you very far.

The *yes* means I accept what exists — something someone says or does, an objection, my slides not working … bedbugs.

The *and* means I will use what exists and offer something back.

No vs. Yes

Often, the impulse is to lead with a "no" or "yes, but" (which is really what Kat's mentor Cal Sutliff used to call a "designer no"). Why is this? Sometimes it's simply

---

56 Brown, P., and Levinson, S. C. (1987). *Politeness: Some Universals in Language Usage*. Cambridge University Press.

habitual. David Kelley, founder of IDEO, started the innovation center because as an engineering professor at Stanford, he said he had the smartest people in the world in his classes, but they thought that being smart meant shooting holes in other people's ideas.

Keith Johnstone, the author of *Impro: Improvisation and the Theatre*[57] and a seminal improvisational theater director, says, "There are people who prefer to say 'yes,' and people who prefer to say 'no.' People who say 'yes' are rewarded by the adventures they have. People who say 'no' are rewarded by the safety they attain." While choosing to say "no" may offer a sense of security, it often comes at the cost of missing out on potential adventures, personal development, and the valuable lessons that come with navigating uncharted territory.

Both as participants and as facilitators ourselves, our habits and our self-protective instincts can lead us to blocking rather than accepting offers. And don't get us wrong: Safety is great. There are legitimate reasons to say no. (William Ury, coauthor of the pivotal negotiation book *Getting to Yes*,[58] later wrote a book called *The Power of a Positive No*,[59] because he speculated about what he had done, since everyone was agreeing in ways that hurt their own interests.) But when we can flex our capacity to consciously and courageously choose yes or no, rather than just habitually react out of self-protection (or mindless agreement), we up our ability to connect and build with others.

---

57 Johnstone, K. (1981). *Impro: Improvisation and the Theatre* (1st ed.). Methuen Drama.
58 Fisher, R., and Ury, W. (1981). Getting to Yes: Negotiating Agreement Without Giving In (1st ed.). Penguin Books.
59 Ury, W. (2007). The Power of a Positive No: Save the Deal, Save the Relationship and Still Say No (1st ed.). Bantam.

For example, you say, "Let's fix the order entry process." Some folks immediately raise objections. Others lean into the idea, accepting and building with it. Although all of the issues on the "yes, but" side might be valid, can you see how accepting and building with the initial offer opens up possibilities as opposed to shutting them down?

"Let's fix the order entry process."	
"Yes, but ..."	**"Yes, and ..."**
"Yes, but we don't have the resources to do it."	"Yes, and with a solid business case, we could get the needed resources."
"Yes, but the bigger problem is our ERP system."	"Yes, and it could highlight the need for more changes."
"Yes, but customers like it the way it is."	"Yes, and we could get the 'voice of the customer' as we work on improvements."
"Yes, but we have too much on our plates now."	"Yes, and it could make our lives easier, so we don't feel overloaded all the time."

As a facilitator and leader, especially, here's why it's worth building the "Yes, and" habit:

Giving Control = More Collaboration

We like being in the driver's seat of conversations, especially when we're focused on the outcome we want or we're the subject-matter expert. With a "Yes, and" mindset, we open up the possibility of co-creating solutions because people are more motivated to work with us. The Self-Determination Theory[60] suggests that one way to unlock people's motivation is to help them

---

60 Deci, E. L., and Ryan, R. M. (1985). *Intrinsic Motivation and Self-Determination in Human Behavior*. Plenum.

feel competent. When you acknowledge and build on a person's idea, it increases their confidence, connection, and affiliation with you. It's like sharing the driver's wheel versus relegating people to the backseat and assuming they'll come along for the ride.

Openness Leads to Innovation

"Yes, and" is a conversational lubricant. When you listen first and build on people's offers, they are more willing to engage with you and open up more possibilities. Design Thinking, an iterative process for problem-solving, highlights this idea. A core step of Design Thinking is ideation where the goal is to challenge assumptions and create new, innovative ideas.

"Yes, and" promotes an open mindset while tamping down the urge to criticize or discount ideas. Great minds don't think alike. Teams that are cognitively diverse, meaning there are differences in perspectives or information processing, solve problems faster.[61] This is especially true in new, uncertain, and complex situations. A "Yes, and" mentality promotes the sharing of new ideas and ways of thinking.

Breaks Our No Habit

Ironically, the more power and decision-making authority we acquire, the more safety and protecting our way of doing things can subversively seep into our practice. Those in control already can tend toward a habitual no.

---

61 Reynolds, A., and Lewis, D. (2017). Teams Solve Problems Faster When They're More Cognitively Diverse. Harvard Business Review.

Sometimes we value the status quo and not opportunity. Meaning, if you say yes, it may mean more work for you, another person's idea will move forward, they get more recognition, and you'll have to do something in a new way that threatens your sense of comfort and safety.

Deepen Understanding

If you aren't able to find an offer you can authentically respond to with "Yes, and" at first, consider getting curious and uncovering more offers before reverting to a no.

Alternatives to No
"Tell me more about that."
"Help me understand what I may be missing."
"Take me through your thought process."
"Connect the dots for me."

When to Say No

If your child says, "I'm going to play in the street," we don't recommend replying, "Yes, and take the dog with you!" If your boss says, "I need you to falsely inflate your expense report." We don't advocate saying, "Yes, and I can alter my timecard, too!"

We all have personal standards and principles that shouldn't be crossed — such as safety, ethics, values, and beliefs — and we're not advocating you compromise on them. When that happens, recognize you are always saying yes to something larger. Saying no to the boss means you're saying yes to your ethics. Saying no to your child playing in the street means you're saying yes to safety and parental control.

In (ideally) most situations where your principles are not being compromised but you disagree with a person, start by acknowledging shared values or feelings. For instance, your child might have pent-up energy and because you were working all day, you didn't spend time with them. You could respond, "I know you've been cooped up all day. Playing in the street isn't an option. How about we go to the park instead?"

Stay true to your core intentions

• Say "yes" to your values and mission.

• Say "yes" to exploring other positions that can meet mutual interest.

• Say "no" to positions that are incompatable.

Imagine a tree with roots representing values, intentions, and goals. Someone's idea comes along and cuts down the trunk. What can you accept and build on so the tree can keep growing? For instance, maybe now isn't the right time to fix the order entry process and we don't have the budget, but you can accept the value of making things better or acknowledge frustration over a broken process. Maybe you could respond with "Yes, and" the value of being committed to each other even though resources are limited.

No vs. Yes in Practice

Nigel discovered one of his client's business units was still relying on legacy accounting systems, which meant reports were manually generated and ripe for quality issues. He saw an opportunity to discuss (and then sell) an improvement to Radhika, the client. He scheduled the meeting and titled it Digital Transformation.

Nigel: "Hi, Radhika."

Radhika: "Hi. I see you want to talk about digital transformation, but I already know our reporting systems are antiquated."

Nigel: "That's normal. Sometimes parts of the company adopt new software solutions faster than others. The good news is that there's a new software platform that can really lower cost and streamline the process."

Radhika: "I can't really think about that right now. We have to get through this fiscal year. Plus, we have other major initiatives happening and — "

Nigel: "Of course! Of course, but better systems could help you solve some of your bigger problems."

Radhika: "I'll stop you right there. It's more complicated than you realize. We're in the midst of acquiring another business and the budget for some of our transformation projects got redirected to that."

Well, that didn't go great for Nigel, did it? He was presenting a solution and missed Radhika's offers. When focusing on our own ideas, needs, and expertise, we filter out anything that doesn't seem to serve our purpose and the conversation doesn't advance.

Nigel didn't mean to undermine connection and communication, so what happened?

1. Nigel had a purpose in mind (digital transformation) and stuck with it, which meant he simply missed offers. As we mention in the "Listening" chapter, noticing is hard. Some of Radhika's offers were:

   - She knows the systems are old but wants to prioritize "first things first."

   - She wants to avoid the topic because it's "complicated."

   - The budget was redirected to the acquisition.

2. Nigel worried that if he accepted and pursued Radhika's offers, he would be demonstrating agreement. Radhika feels the topic is complicated, and it may or may not be. If Nigel accepts that she thinks it's complicated, will she think he agrees that it's too complicated to address?

3. Nigel, like those Stanford engineering students, equates looking smart with debating or blocking others.

Let's imagine Nigel gets a do-over. This time, his goal will be to notice offers and find ways to accept and build with them.

Radhika: "Yes, I know our systems are antiquated."

Nigel: "What are you experiencing?" or "Sounds like it's on your radar. Tell me more."

Radhika: "I can't even think about digital transformation right now. We have to get through this fiscal year. Plus, we have other major initiatives happening."

Nigel: "It sounds like your plate is very full. What are your top priorities?"

When you contribute to a conversation this way, you demonstrate a willingness to follow their lead and have the conversation they want to have. You discover advantages and resources otherwise overlooked or dismissed. Adapting for impact empowers us to create in the midst of uncertainty, to flex as the ground shakes, and to keep moving forward. It's generating solutions based on what actually exists, whether or not conditions are favorable and expected.

The first version is more likely to lead to unproductive debate and stalemate. In the second conversation, if digital transformation is a useful project in the current environment, Nigel, by accepting and building with Radhika's concerns, will help them both discover how it supports her main goals and eases other issues. If the time is not right, Nigel has saved himself and Radhika's time and energy while uncovering other opportunities.

Try This: 'Yes And'

Think of a recent situation when you said no. As a result, what were you saying yes to?

List reasons why you might block offers ("No" or "Yes, but").

(For example, someone you don't like champions the idea, the idea feels risky, you like your idea better, you don't recognize an offer is being made, saying yes means more work for you.)

Practice "Yes, and" in lower-risk situations. What is an upcoming moment when you can intentionally accept and build on an offer?

(For example, your friend suggests eating at a Mexican restaurant while you crave Italian food. You reply, "Yes, and let's get dessert at that new gelato place.")

Handling Questions

Fielding questions is a key moment in which serving purpose is put to the test, and our capacity to notice, accept, and build with offers lies at the heart of doing it well.

"What time is the 3:00 parade?"

It's one of the most common questions Walt Disney cast members get from guests.[62] On the surface, there's

---

62 How Would You Respond If Asked: 'What Time Is The 3 O'clock Parade?' (2018, December 11) Disney Institute Blog https://www.disneyinstitute.com/blog/how-would-you-respond-if-asked-what-time-is-the-3-oclock-parade/

an obvious answer, but cast members know there's a question *behind* that question. What guests are really wondering is, "What time will the 3:00 parade get to *me*?" or "Where should I stand to get the best view?" It's an important moment because how a cast member responds to the question determines whether the exchange will end abruptly or become a positive experience.

Questions require us to flex because they can often feel like challenges to our content, our agenda, and our knowledge. When we're asked a question, the default for most people is to answer it directly, which can be a way to demonstrate credibility and subject-matter knowledge. That's a good choice when people are looking for a simple answer, yet, it can be a missed opportunity for a better exchange and may even lower your credibility.

Answering directly assumes you know why the question is being asked. There's often more under the surface of a question especially when you can pick up on more context clues, like the tone, body language, and the current environment. Here are some examples.

What's Asked	What's under the Surface
Is senior leadership participating, too?	Is this just lip service or will they really walk the talk?
How much does it cost?	My boss is the decision-maker and our budget just got slashed.
Is this similar to the XL580 product launch?	I know a lot about this topic and I want you to know it, too.
How do you think customers will respond to the new pricing structure?	I *know* customers are going to hate it. I want to see if you understand the implications.

If you answered the "surface" question ("Yes." "$2,500." "Very similar." "I'm not sure."), you miss the point. It's in those moments that people decide to continue to engage or not.

Most questions fall into three types:

 Looking for information ("Have you worked with other clients like us?")

 Expressing a concern ("Can we *really* count on that deadline?")

 A point of view in the form of a question ("Don't you think it would be better to wait until next fiscal year?")

Anticipate Questions

Colette was a newly promoted marketing manager, and her new responsibility was presenting the story of her investment firm to prospective clients. She thought she was prepared, having rehearsed multiple times. She felt confident — until the client asked some unexpected questions, which disrupted her train of thought. Flustered, her answers were either too long and detailed or didn't address the questions. With Colette's confidence shaken, the managing director had to step in to respond until she could find her footing again.

It's impossible to predict every question you might get, particularly when interacting with new people. However, you can prepare by temporarily stepping into their shoes and imagining what's important to them. For instance, if you're meeting with a client who has been in the news over a recent data privacy breach, consider what questions might arise from their current reality.

Answer the Question

The process of responding to a question is as important as the answer.

Confirm Your Understanding

When you receive a loaded question with an implied answer (such as "Is it really going to cost that much?"), resist the urge to defend or debate. Instead, restate your understanding of what might be under the surface. It might be: "It's a bigger investment than you were expecting, and you want to know why" or "You're wondering how we arrived at that number." Reframing the question through a restatement allows you to approach the answer with more confidence and clarity. Visit the "Listen" chapter for more about the skill of restating.

Pause

Watch any professional debate or Supreme Court Justice confirmation process and you'll notice this common denominator. Especially when receiving a tough question or being put on the spot, give yourself a moment to breathe, collect your thoughts, and consider how to frame your reply. "That's an interesting question, let me take a second to think about it" can be an acceptable answer. It demonstrates thoughtfulness, which lends credibility to your answer. Like anything, though, don't over-rely on it.

Be Succinct

If your child asks, "Where do babies come from?," you have a choice. Depending on their age, maturity, and level of curiosity, your answer might range from the very simple and literal, "The hospital," to a more biologically accurate answer.

In general, providing a short answer to questions is the best option, especially when it's included with a check for completeness, like, "Does that answer your question?" Giving long, rambling answers doesn't build your credibility. Too much detail just tends to confuse people. Even worse, it may plant seeds of doubt about the validity of your answers if you ramble.

Three-Dimensionalize Your Answer

"Would it help if I gave an example?" It's one of our favorite responses when answering complex questions or ones that require a nuanced answer. A story or example provides proof and legitimacy to the answer. It makes it more likely for the questioner to understand and relate to the answer rather than just relying on facts or data. Refer to the "Engage with Story" chapter for the skills of how to craft stories that make a big impact.

Giving a direct answer to questions isn't the only option. The more you know your options, the more you can adapt for impact.

Here are alternatives to directly answering a question.

Open the Question to Others

Invite others to respond, especially when there's more than one right answer. For instance, if the question is "How do you get customers to change their behavior?," you could crowdsource the answer by saying, "I know others have faced that challenge, too. Let's generate some ideas. What are others doing that's working?" The value of tossing back the question is that it drives a group conversation instead of being an exchange only with you. It recognizes the wisdom in the room, and when people feel appreciated and valued, they contribute more.

Another bonus of tossing the question to the group is that you don't always need to have an answer. But do it with caution. Over-relying on this option can leave people thinking you don't have *any* answers. A mix of approaches is best.

Create a Parking Lot

Not all great questions need an answer on the spot. For instance, you are facilitating a discussion about the three-year strategy and you get a question about how to resolve a current but important client problem. It's a great question and you might think it will be easy to answer it quickly. Before you know it, though, what was intended as a one-minute answer has turned into a ten-minute discussion.

When you get a question, filter it for relevance and decide if you're at the right time to answer it. Ask yourself, *Will it serve the group if we discuss this?* If the answer is no, respectfully offer to put it in a parking lot and then return to it later or take it off-line. (A parking lot might be writing the question on a whiteboard or making a note.)

Admit You Don't Know

For some, this may feel like the last option and for others it's a comfortable option. People experience you as relatable and human when you admit to not having all the answers. Saying "I don't know" reflects your intellectual humility.[63] Recognizing the limits of your knowledge demonstrates an openness to other people's knowledge and an appreciation that no one knows it all. When you hold a position of power (for example, you are the subject-matter expert or the most senior person), the more you stay open to expressing what you don't know, the more connection and credibility you build with those who hold less power.

63 Porter, T., and Schuman, K (2018). Intellectual humility and openness to the opposing view, Self and Identity 17:2, 139–162, doi: 10.1080/15298868.2017.1361861.

Try This: Anticipate Questions

While you can't prepare and rehearse for every curve ball you might encounter, you can build the ability to flex quickly, no matter the situation.

Before your next meeting, think about the participants. What questions can you anticipate and how will you respond?

Addressing Objections and Resistance

"I don't want to be here. My boss made me come."

"That's not going to work."

"It costs too much."

Objections, like questions, can be triggering. There isn't one magical solution for handling pushback, but a good start is to employ deep D.I.V.E. listening and seek to uncover offers you can accept and build with. We explained this concept in the previous chapter.

Alexi spent days preparing for his meeting with Shanice, who was becoming certified in a conflict management approach. When he shared the agenda with her, he was caught off-guard when Shanice said, "Really? I don't think this will work for me. I'd rather see you give more examples and then walk me through it and, and, and ...." In essence, she was asking Alexi to go on a different route than what he planned. As he felt his face turn red, he was at a "Serve the Purpose" crossroads before they even started. He could say, "What I designed is the best, most efficient, and proven way to do it if you want to get certified." If he took that approach, he could expect malicious or resentful compliance at best, but not real buy-in.

When you are the facilitator, it can feel like the rug is being pulled from under you when faced with pushback, yet being dogmatic about the agenda or process risks alienating people and never reaching the desired outcome.

Alexi took a deep breath and stayed curious. He said, "Tell me more about how you'd like to approach it." She went into more detail and he listened intently, then restated her need: "You want to walk through more scenarios and what-if situations."

> **Supportive Self-Talk When the Unexpected Happens**
> - "It's not what I could have anticipated, but I'll stay curious."
> - "Visible resistance means we can address it openly."
> - "No matter what I hear, I'll accept and build on it."
> - "Focus on what the group needs now."
> - "This will make for a good story one day!"

She nodded and he replied, "Okay, we can go that route, provided you're able to demonstrate X, Y, and Z by the end of tomorrow." They both agreed. In the end, Alexi didn't let go of the end goal — just the path to get there. It wasn't his preferred path, but he was willing to take Shanice's path for the benefit of the relationship and a smoother path to the outcome, which they both wanted.

When you encounter a situation where you get pushback on the agenda or your meeting approach, try to do this:

Give choice. There's often more than one way to reach a goal. Stay open to alternative ways to get there.

Give control. When people feel they have some agency in how a process or meeting will work, they are more likely to be invested and committed versus passively participating.

Acknowledge It

When someone objects, rather than blocking them by arguing or getting defensive, invite the person to express their thoughts without interruption. Show that you've listened to their concerns by restating your understanding. By doing so, you demonstrate respect for the person and send a strong signal to others that they have an open and safe environment to speak their truth.

Involve Others

In a group setting, invite others to weigh in. Therese was leading a meeting with a group of managers when one spoke up and said, "I don't think we need help with our strategy. We've already figured it out." Instead of debating it or claiming that she had all the answers, Therese tested the comment with the group, asking, "Do others feel this way?" Then others expressed why the team needed the help. Instead of Therese needing to convince the dissenter, the group convinced him of the value.

This approach not only fosters a sense of inclusivity and ownership within the group, but also allows diverse perspectives to be heard and considered. By inviting others to weigh in, you empower the team to collaborate and solve the obstacle.

Find Common Ground

Fighting people's resistance is like trying to swim upstream against a powerful current: No matter how hard you struggle, you find yourself making little progress and expending tremendous energy.

When you don't see eye to eye, seek common ground or shared objectives. Highlight the mutual goals or values that you can align on. By focusing on shared interests, you can create the path to a solution.

After the Meeting

The end is just the beginning. Most of us have been in meetings where there's lots of passion and energy at the moment, only to see it fizzle afterward. The challenge of keeping on track intensifies now because it relies on individuals (usually with competing priorities) to keep commitments. Whether you own some action items or your work with the group is done, you'll continue to add value by creating a glide path for progress.

Summarize Meeting Output

People's memories fade fast. Create (or assign someone) to create a summary of action items, owners, and deliverables — and send it out quickly. Confirm that this captures everyone's understanding. It's better to know at this early stage if people have a different recollection or if something has changed.

Offer Support

A group can easily fall off the track if there isn't a regular cadence of progress check-ins. Support can come in many forms, from arranging the next meeting to one-on-one conversations. Balance holding people accountable with accepting mistakes and misfires. When people aren't held accountable for their commitments, the team loses steam and performance is inconsistent. Likewise, when it's not safe to discuss a mistake or a problem, people withhold information and facts, and progress stalls.

Keep Learning: Ask for and Give Feedback

Check in with the meeting sponsor or participants to learn what worked effectively and what got in the way. Simply asking "How do you think it went?" usually won't get you much in the way of useful feedback. To elicit more detail, ask, "What did you like about how that meeting worked, what concerns do you have, and what suggestions do you have for next time?"

Everyone has a role in making the quality of meetings better. At times, it means giving people feedback about how they helped or hindered meeting progress. For instance, if you noticed someone helped others keep on track or create space for others to speak up, acknowledge their positive impact. Likewise, if someone talks over others or discounts people's opinions, that's worth noting in a private moment with them. Check out the "Support People's Development" chapter for an effective way to frame your message, whether positive or corrective, and deliver it in a way that people are likely to accept.

Try This: Keep on Track

Put the keeping-on-track skills to use.

- Pick an upcoming meeting that's relatively low risk and where people will accept your offer to facilitate (maybe a monthly meeting, project review call, or lunch-and-learn topic).

- How will you get agreement about how the group will work together?

- Consider what tends to take this group off-track (such as interrupting, invalidating people's perspectives, getting into too much detail). List them.

- Think about what you might say or do to help the group stay on track.

- Note some phrases you might use to call out unhelpful patterns of behavior.

Serving the Purpose Is Everyone's Job

In this chapter, we focused on how to guide groups toward their desired outcomes. It might be easy to assume these are skills reserved for the meeting leader or official facilitator, but that's not true. When every participant sees it as their responsibility to keep the group focused, meetings become more productive and enjoyable. If you join a meeting and there's no clear agenda or process, ask for it. When the group gets bogged down in too much detail, call it out and offer an idea for getting back on track. Use the F.I.T. filter as groups agree on action items. You can have a bigger impact, from any seat, by using these skills.

Chapter Takeaways

- When faced with the choices to stick to the agenda or going off-roading, ask yourself: What's in the best service of the group right now? Sometimes, it's a detour; other times, stick to the plan.

- Start with clarifying the purpose and goal of your meeting. Those will inform the agenda, who should be invited (or not invited), and roles and responsibilities.

- When groups seem stuck, carefully listen to what's causing the obstacle, and then name it for the group's benefit. Flex to the needs of the group while keeping the objectives in clear view.

- By consciously and courageously choosing between yes or no, rather than habitually reacting out of self-protection or mindless agreement, we enhance our ability to build trust, generate ideas, and solve problems.

- Questions may feel like challenges to our knowledge and agenda, but it can be an opportunity for better exchanges. Listen below the surface and know your options.

- When encountering pushback, offer choices for achieving the goal and give control to encourage active participation and commitment.

10 Balance Risk and Safety

Provide the right level of support and challenge to the individual and group.

I assess what's needed to increase feelings of safety or reduce perceived risks.

I create opportunities to stretch and explore new possibilities without fear of shame or punishment.

I ensure everyone feels safe in expressing their perspectives.

I model and acknowledge vulnerability.

On a scale of 1 to 10, how risky is skydiving? How about giving a speech to a thousand strangers? Walking home alone at night? What about managing a classroom of seven-year-olds? Asking your boss for a raise? Saying no to your biggest client?

How would your best friend answer these questions? Your teammate? Your boss? Your mom? We are pretty certain they would each rate those situations differently. While our brains are wired to sense safety and risk, that internal warning system is unique to us.[64] What you find scary may be easy and comfortable for others and vice versa.

---

64 Brown, V.J. (2014). Risk perception: it's personal. *Environmental Health Perspectives* 122(10):A276-9. doi: 10.1289/ehp.122-A276. PMID: 25272337; PMCID: PMC4181910.

Early in her career, Therese's boss asked her to fill in for him at a senior staff meeting. He thought he was giving a low-risk request and responded to her hesitancy with reassurances like, "Don't worry." "You'll be fine." "This is a great opportunity for you!" That did not assuage her fears. She worried she wasn't prepared enough and equally concerned about her boss's perception if she told him she didn't feel ready. He had no clue that she lost sleep and was stressed about it for days. We often fail to spot the signs of people's comfort level and misjudge how they perceive risk.

Initially, when we worked with groups, we focused mostly on how to foster a sense of safety. We wanted people to be at ease when working with us. But soon we realized that safety is only half the equation. The more advanced skill is balancing risk and safety, because it is equally important to know when and how to apply the gentle pressure that prompts people out of their comfort zones — that's where growth happens. The questions we asked ourselves are: How can we sense and respond[65] to people's perception of risk? How can we help people get comfortable being uncomfortable when the situation calls for it?

Feeling Safe

Amy Edmondson, the Novartis Professor of Leadership and Management at the Harvard Business School, popularized the concept of psychological safety. She defined it as "a shared belief held by members of a team that the team is safe for interpersonal risk taking."

---

65 Haecke, S. H. (1999). *Adaptive Enterprise: Creating and Leading Sense-And-Respond Organizations.* Harvard Business Review Press.

We still have a long way to go to truly understand and realize psychological safety. In a 2021 *Harvard Business Review* article,[66] Edmondson wrote, "One crucial misconception among business leaders is that psychological safety will be present in any reasonably healthy work environment, like freedom from harassment or a commitment to keeping workers injury-free. In fact, psychologically safe work environments are rare."

Timothy R. Clark, author of *The Four Stages of Psychological Safety*,[67] defines psychological safety as a condition in which you feel (1) included, (2) safe to learn, (3) safe to contribute, and (4) safe to challenge the status quo — all without fear of being embarrassed, marginalized, or punished in some way.

To be clear, good facilitation alone cannot magically and immediately resolve complex and difficult group dynamics. However, we can still equip ourselves with the skills to diagnose what is required in any given situation and make choices that help dial down the risk quotient.

Sometimes you can tell when people in a group feel safe because their bodies and behaviors are clear indicators. Typically, you'll see smiling, laughter, a relaxed posture, and people speaking freely and candidly. Beyond that, people will be publicly vulnerable, acknowledging mistakes and difficulties, along with a willingness to take a risk or try something new.

Take Luca, for example. New to the company, he was attending his first quarterly operations meeting. He

66 Edmondson, A.C, and Hugander P. (2021, June 22). 4 Steps to Boost Psychological Safety at Your Workplace. Harvard Business Review (HBR.org).
67 Clark, T. (2020). *The Four Stages of Psychological Safety.* Berrett-Koehler.

noticed a striking difference between his new workplace and his previous one. Here, people weren't afraid to voice opposing points of view.

During a key decision-making moment, when the team appeared to have reached consensus, Tiffany spoke up. "I don't mean to slow the momentum, but we're not addressing the biggest issue here," she said. The team listened and stayed curious without shutting her down. This was possible because of the safe environment they had created. Otherwise, she might not have had the courage to speak up and the decision wouldn't have been stress-tested to the same degree.

Later in the meeting, the team needed someone to test out a new approach in front of everyone. Evan stepped up, saying, "I'll do it. I might fall on my face, but I'm willing to see how it works!"

He made several mistakes. The senior-most person in the room lightened the mood, saying, "Well, that didn't work, but I don't think I could have done any better!" The team responded with collective laughter and appreciation for Evan's willingness to experiment. This is the power of a psychologically safe team — the fear of failure is dialed down, and members feel comfortable taking risks, trying new things, and learning from their mistakes.

Statements that Support Safety

- "We haven't heard from everyone yet. What do others think?"
- "That perspective isn't reflective of everyone's experience."
- "It sounds like you are making an assumption."
- That comment can be offensive. Can you state it in a different way or clarify what you mean?"

To dial up the safety quotient, people need to feel valued, respected, and connected to the group. It's our job to observe, point out, and address exclusionary or inappropriate behavior that erodes a sense of safety. Notice how under-represented groups, in particular, experience group interactions where inequities and power dynamics are at play. For instance, a person's name being consistently mispronounced or misspelled, a person being ignored in a meeting, not using a person's correct pronouns, or someone diminishing another's lived experience all reduce their sense that they can trust the environment and the people in it are safe. You create safety, and act as an ally, when you notice and then address it in the moment.

Try This: Sensing Safety

What makes me feel safe?

What can I do to help others feel safe?

Tolerating Risk

"Comfort and growth do not coexist."

Ginni Rometty, former chairwoman,
president and CEO, IBM

We hire personal trainers expecting to sweat. In this scenario, we don't misinterpret our stress and fatigue as bad signs. Rather, we see how the "pain" leads to "gain": We are getting a good workout and building strength. In much the same way, leaders are tasked with helping people and teams stretch and grow. And just like personal trainers, we must know how far to stretch the limits. Overdoing it can cause injury and resentment, and going too easy results in wasted time and effort.

Balancing the risk side of the equation means creating the conditions in which people can feel comfortable being uncomfortable. Risk might take the form of a manager awkwardly (but bravely!) practicing a new skill for the first time, a colleague calling out a sexist comment made in a meeting, a person making a difficult and unpopular decision, or the leader being vulnerable and admitting a mistake.

Teams that work through obstacles together and face more adversity become closer and higher-performing than those that operate in status quo environments.[68] Whether it is a battalion fighting an enemy on the battlefield or a software team facing a difficult technical problem under time pressure, we tend to form greater

---

68 Bastian, B., Jetten, J., Thai, H. A., and Steffens, N. K. (2018). Shared Adversity Increases Team Creativity Through Fostering Supportive Interaction. *Frontiers in Psychology Volume 9*, 383816. https://doi.org/10.3389/fpsyg.2018.02309.

connections and stronger bonds when we face risk together — even reliving those moments together with pride.

This contribution requires good detective skills because, as we mentioned before, people have varying levels of risk tolerance. Understanding how others perceive risk is key. For example, if you're trying to persuade a skeptical colleague to adopt a new process, being able to recognize and address risk perception is critical.

It can feel risky to talk about risk. In our experience, people don't readily volunteer what they find uncomfortable and dangerous unless they are very self-aware and in a trusting (safe) relationship. The signs can be subtle (the client rescheduling the meeting for the third time or staying silent on a call) to more obvious (your colleague telling you, "I'm not comfortable with that approach").

Think of those signs as the tip of an iceberg — to get to the bottom of people's hesitancy, you need to explore what's under the surface. The number one skill to help you do it is listening. As we explored in the "Listen" chapter, asking questions is a powerful tool in seeing the entire picture from the other person's point of view. Restate their concerns — even if you don't agree with them, acknowledge their reality. Until people believe you understand and empathize with their concerns, they won't be open to hearing your prescription for risk reduction.

1. See the Signs of Resistance

- Choosing words carefully
- Avoiding eye contact
- Stiffer body language (arms crossed, flat facial expression, rigid posture)
- Inaction or delay a decision
- Avoidance (e.g., not attending meetings)
- Excuses (e.g., "This doesn't really apply to me or my team.")
- Statements that signal risk ("We might not make the quarter if we add one more thing to our plate.")

See the Signs

Explore beneath the surface

2. Explore Beneath the Surface

- "What's getting in the way?"
- "What's making you hesitant to make a decision?"
- "Tell me more about your concerns."

Restate (Verbalize your understanding of *their* perspective)

- "You're worried the team isn't ready for the change."
- "It's risky to try and pull this off in the last quarter."
- "We need senior leadership buy-in before investing more time."

Try This: Sensing Risk

What makes me feel at risk?

Think about your colleagues or clients. What behaviors tell you they feel at risk?

Risk and Safety Conversations

Imagine a conversation between Celia, head of HR, and Anton, CEO of Spark, a mid-sized financial services company. Anton asked for some support in getting everyone to work in the office five days a week. For months, he bemoaned people abusing the hybrid work policy and crowed about how working face-to-face promotes more innovative problem-solving and esprit de corps.

Celia knew, however, that most employees had no desire to work from the office full-time. A significant majority said they felt more productive and even more engaged and motivated when working remotely. Moreover, competitors in the field were providing more flexibility by working remotely. For Spark to retain talent in their market, all the future-of-work trends pointed toward hybrid work options. If Anton couldn't change his mindset, Spark would be at a significant disadvantage.

How might Celia think about risk and safety as she prepares for her conversation with Anton? First, she will assess risk and safety for herself, and what Anton might be feeling. She realizes that what feels high-stakes or uncomfortable to her may not be what Anton experiences.

Here are four possible types of conversations that assessment yields:

Comfotable Conversation

Familiar and Relaxed

Comfortable Conversations: These are low risk for all parties. For instance, you're giving a status update on a routine project to a trusted, long-standing colleague. These interactions are relaxed and congenial.

Get-Out-Of-Your-Own-Way Conversations

Comfortable for others, uncomfortable for you

Get-Out-of-Your-Own-Way Conversations: These conversations might feel risky to you, but others may find them comfortable and even welcome. For instance, your colleague might be open to feedback and actively seek it from you, but due to a past negative experience with a former co-worker, you hesitate to provide it.

Take Care Conversations

Comfortable for you, uncomfortable for them

Take Care Conversations: You welcome these conversations but they feel risky or uncomfortable for others. As an example you are on the team that's revamping the antiquated commission structure for the sales force. The sales leaders on the team are concerned it's too big a change this year.

Brave Conversations
Uncomfortable for you and them

Brave Conversations: These are the conversations where everyone is navigating risky and potentially uncomfortable topics. It's often the easiest to avoid, but potentially the most fruitful, such as a conversation with your boss about perceived gender bias in the team. Often, the path to these conversations travels through a Comfortable or Get-Out-of-Your-Own-Way conversation — just one extra conscious step into a little bit of discomfort-building on the next and the next, growing braver as they go.

Managing Risk and Safety Conversations

Comfortable Conversations: Most of us do whatever we can to live in the land of Comfortable Conversations — and with good reason. If all conversations felt risky, it would make for endlessly stressful days.

When to Have
- Establishing a new relationship
- Maintaining the status quo
- Returning to comfort – when previous conversations have felt risky to both of you

Tips for Managing
- Acknowledge the value – show appreciation
- Check to ensure these conversations are still of value
- Be fully present
- Ask: What are we not talking about or avoiding?

When we're forming a new relationship or building rapport, we'll often start here as a way to warm up to each other. Also, these conversations can be a refuge after many riskier discussions. The routine and predictability of Comfortable Conversations serve as a relationship breather.

Yet, if all conversations are safe, there's often a missed opportunity for progress. When you are having mostly safe, comfortable conversations, it is worth taking a moment to ask, "Am I maximizing my opportunities? Where might I challenge myself? Where might I stretch my client's interest and commitments?"

In Celia and Anton's case, this conversation could be any number of things from how frustrating COVID is to how someday work life will get back to normal to conversations about current P&L statements. Sometimes Comfortable Conversations build rapport and allow you to cover necessary ground with ease. But in the face of an important issue like the one Anton is facing, settling for a Comfortable Conversation seems, at best, a missed opportunity and, at worst, conflict avoidance.

Get-Out-of-Your-Own-Way Conversations: Coming from a struggling artist and nonprofit background, Kat realized she felt shy discussing money. The dollar amounts being casually tossed around in corporate training and consulting circles were orders of magnitude outside her norms, so she would avoid pricing conversations for as long as possible. When she did quote a price, she would surround it with disclaimers like, "We never want price to be an obstacle to working together" or "Of course, we're flexible; just let us know your budget."

Sometimes, that approach worked out just fine; Kat could justify her avoidance as a savvy strategy for building rapport and establishing value. After all, clients were concerned about price and her comments addressed that obstacle, right? Eventually, however, Kat faced the fact that most of her clients were very comfortable with conversations about price and it was her own anxiety that she needed to manage, not theirs.

Once she confronted this truth, she could identify her negative self-talk and work to reframe it from "They will think this is too expensive" to "We have set our rates thoughtfully and we deserve to be compensated for our expertise."

When you are uncomfortable with a conversation, start by managing the voice in your head. Revisit the "Manage Yourself" chapter for a step-by-step on how to do it. Then practice delivering your message — either recruit a friend or confidant or practice in a mirror.

When to Have

• You're avoiding a necessary but vital conversation out of your own fear.
• It benefits both parties.

Tips for Managing

• Manage your self-talk.
• Acknowledge your discomfort.
• Practice having the conversation with a friend first.

Take Care Conversations: These conversations are about strengthening trust and empathy to guide people into riskier waters. In our earlier example, Celia recognizes that her conversation with Anton will be a Take Care Conversation. Discussing the future of work is exciting for her because she's feels really good about all the new possibilities for attracting the best talent to Spark. However, she knows Anton feels threatened by the idea. Therefore, she will tread carefully by listening to him first and demonstrating empathy for his perspective.

Although she is confident about jumping straight into action, she won't be stringent or dogmatic, staying calm and explicitly stating the value and benefits of exploring the topic. Celia is clear, as she guides Anton through this territory that feels new and dangerous to him, to prove her trustworthiness along the way.

Take Care Conversations
Comfortable for you; uncomfortable for them

When to Have
- Your expertise is valued
- Your motive is known
- There's mutual respect

Tips for Managing
- Listen with empathy
- Acknowledge their discomfort
- Offer options
- Go slow; recognize progress
- State the value for having the conversation (hoped-for outcomes)

Brave Conversations: Like a band of heroes lost in an enchanted forest in a fantasy adventure story, you and the other person must depend on each other to find your way. Neither of you quite knows the territory; neither of you knows exactly what will come next. But if trust is high and you commit to diving into uncharted territory in search of greater value, it is almost always there to find. Start by acknowledging the situation and distinguish between exploration ("Let's just get on the same page today") versus commitment ("We need to make a decision now"). Focus on shared values[69] and desired outcomes to find the path together.

Roger, the vice president of marketing, received troubling feedback that he wasn't an inclusive leader. A big golfer, he hosted "optional" after-work golf events at his country club. Informal but important business discussions happened on the golf course and this put the non-golfers, who happened to be the women and people of color on his team, in a bind. Not attending meant unequal access to those important conversations and less visibility and relationship-building with Roger.

69 Satell, G. and Windschitl, C. (2021, May 11). High Performing Teams Start with a Culture of Shared Values. Harvard Business Review. (HBR.org)

Some non-golfers attended, but Roger seemed oblivious to their discomfort. After a few days of reflection, he realized he had some unconscious bias and then worried he was a bad person. It called into question how else he might be perpetuating systemic bias.

He invited his direct reports, Caitlyn and Geoffrey, to a meeting, but they were unsure what he wanted from them. At first, the awkwardness was palpable. Roger, embarrassed and worried he'd get defensive, stumbled over his words. Caitlyn and Geoffrey wondered how candid they could be, fearing a backlash.

Roger took a deep breath and started by thanking them and saying, "I recognize this conversation might be difficult and I want you to know that I'm committed to addressing the feedback. I realize my lived experience is very different from yours, and I'm looking for your help in seeing some of my blind spots."

Caitlyn and Geoffrey slowly eased into the conversation and eventually offered other examples of Roger's biases. Only when he acknowledged the behavior nondefensively did they feel comfortable offering deeper, more significant instances of unconscious bias.

Of course, the story can't end there. Roger's actions can encourage or discourage further brave conversations. If Roger does not act on the feedback, Caitlyn and Geoffrey's sense of risk will be dialed up, the likelihood of offering additional feedback will go down, and Roger's blind spots will persist

When to Have

• An unresolved issue persists
• You believe progress is possible
• You are willing to be vulnerable
• Psychological safety exists

Tips for Managing

• Manage your self talk
• Listen with empathy
• Focus on shared values and desired outcomes
• Agree on ground rules
• Acknowledge the discomfort

Try This: Risk and Safety Conversations

Read the scenarios and then identify the type of conversation and how you might approach it.

Conversation 1: Madeline struggles with leading fundraising conversations because she feels it is outside her area of expertise and frankly, she doesn't like asking people for money. Although she went through training to prepare for these discussions, she still quivers her way through them. It makes no difference whether donors are asking to discuss the topic or not, she would rather avoid them. From her point of view, what kind of conversation is this? If you were in Madeline's shoes, what would you do?

Conversation 2: Annette is handing off assistant principal responsibilities to Nick. She's confident he can handle the role because of how well he manages classrooms and how highly regarded he is by other teachers. When she tells him the good news, she's caught off-guard because he gets uncharacteristically quiet and starts to shift in his seat. Although Nick doesn't object, he is not nearly as enthusiastic or engaged as Annette expected. What would be your next step if you were Annette?

Conversation 3: Bhaskar's brother, Arjun, was laid off last year and has been living with Bhaskar and his family since then. At first, Arjun seemed motivated to find a new position and was very social around the house, but since last month, he has mostly stayed in his room and done little to help with chores. Bhaskar is worried. He wants to support his brother and make sure he is okay. He doesn't want to make him feel bad or unwelcome. He is also pretty certain that Arjun will be reluctant to talk about how he's feeling. What type of conversation should Bhaskar prepare for? What would you expect to encounter if you were Bhaskar?

Conversation 4: Ella, Delilah, and Sam ease into their Monday morning team meeting. Sam describes a concern about workload capacity and Delilah and Ella jump in with options for rebalancing workloads for the week. Sam mentions how supported he's feeling. What kind of conversation did the team just have?

Answers: Conversation #1: Get Out of Your Own Way, #2: Take Care, #3: Brave, #4: Comfortable

----

Risk and Safety in Groups

Things can be even more complicated when interacting with groups because the range of safety and risk is broader. Imagine a CEO presenting at a board of directors meeting with widely disparate views about a proposed acquisition or a change leader proposing a go-live date to a department divided about their readiness to launch.

Large Group Interactions

Varying levels of risk

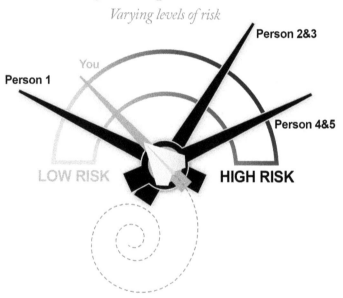

When the complexity increases along with the tension, you have choices for how best to serve the group and the situation.

If you anticipate the situation is going to be challenging, you can reduce the tension before it starts. Here are ways to do so.

BEFORE THE MEETING	DURING THE MEETING	AFTER THE MEETING
• Give advance notice about the topic (avoid surprises). • Meet individually with participants and address issues. • Offer multiple ways of participation (anonymous survey, confidential conversation, etc.).	• Get group agreement on ground rules. • Acknowledge what's happening. • Clarify and summarize different perspectives. • Ensure balanced participation.	• Check-in with people - encourage them to share additional thoughts or concerns privately. • Summarize decisions and timelines. • Schedule a follow-up meeting as needed.

Give people advance notice. No one likes to be caught off-guard. Notifying people in advance allows them to prepare mentally and gather their thoughts.

Meet individually with participants. A conversation before the group meeting can help defuse tension and develop a plan for mitigating feelings of risk.

Offer multiple modes of participation. Therese was facilitating a meeting with a large engineering team who was learning about one of their colleagues transitioning from male to female. The transgender colleague wanted the group to ask her questions, but acknowledged it might be uncomfortable for some. Before the meeting, Therese invited participants to email their questions to her in confidence. Then she shared the questions with the transitioning employee, who felt much more comfortable knowing what was coming and could plan how to address the questions in the meeting.

Fast-forward to the start of the meeting. These choices can help you manage the moment.

Make a group agreement. The rules of the road are especially important in tension-filled situations. Respecting different points of view, listening before judging, and staying curious are examples of possible ground rules. The key is getting agreement and not just passive head nods to those ground rules. When there is true agreement, you can hold the group accountable to them. Visit the "Serve the Purpose" chapter for more on ground rules and group agreement.

Acknowledge what's happening. There's power in naming what's happening in the moment. It serves as a reset for the conversation while demonstrating respect — "There's a real difference of opinion on if we can meet this objective by year end," "We're not on the same page with the implementation plan," or "Some of you are questioning the value of this meeting."

Clarify differing perspectives and look for alternatives for lowering risk. Evelyn, the change project leader, was gearing up for a difficult conversation with the sales team. Craig, VP of sales, wanted to push the go-live date back for a second time while Thomas, the southwest district sales manager, was supportive of implementing it earlier. Bethany, the finance director, was neutral, knowing there was never going to be an ideal time.

Evelyn took a new approach at their meeting. Instead of downplaying Craig's concerns, she invited him to share more about the risks of a temporary slowdown in orders. Then she invited Thomas to share his thinking about how to mitigate the risks. That persuaded Bethany to speak about the value of getting better data in the new system. While the discussion lowered Craig's concerns somewhat, he was still hesitant. Evelyn offered the alternative of implementing in the southwest region first. Bethany was the first to chime in and said, "That's a great idea! Then we can get some early data on how it might work in the rest of the regions."

As the conversation continued, Craig began to feel more comfortable with a phased approach to implementation.

Even the playing field — Ensure balanced participation. Create equity, especially when power dynamics are at play. Our colleague was recently leading a workshop with a mixture of senior- and junior-level people from the same company. A more-senior person pulled our colleague aside and expressed discomfort with talking freely in front of the junior people. He was worried about protecting confidentiality and losing credibility if he had to practice with less-experienced leaders. The fix was to create breakout groups with similar-level people to match status and create more comfort for everyone.

Even when a group agreement is reached, people's sense of safety and risk may still be at odds with one another. After the event, the options may include any of these. :

Check in with people. Provide opportunities for individuals to share additional thoughts or concerns privately, ensuring that their perspectives are considered beyond the immediate discussion.

Summarize decisions and timelines. Sending this information promptly ensures that all participants have a clear record of what was discussed, what has to be accomplished, and by when.

Schedule a follow-up. People might feel the topic is risky, but the relationships are on solid ground. Keeping everyone accountable for their assigned tasks helps ensure that the outcomes of the meeting are effectively implemented.

The most-adept facilitators know they have choices when it comes to balancing risk and safety. It starts with knowing their own level of comfort and then pulling from a range of options to accomplish their goal.

Once we track the perceptions of risk (our own and others'), we can make deliberate choices to turn the comfort dial up or down. Here are some tips for how to increase safety or lean into discomfort, depending on what is needed.

Increasing Safety	
When to	**How to**
• Building or repairing a relationship	• Listen.
• When trust has been broken	• Follow their lead.
• Encouraging people to try something new (break old habits)	• Increase privacy/reinforce confidentiality.
• Power dynamics at play (status)	• Lower the stakes.
• Lowering resistance to change	• Allow silent thinking time.
• A perceived cost/loss to taking the action (risk to credibility, confidence, self-worth)	• Show vulnerability.
	• Show empathy.
	• Celebrate mistake/failure as a path to getting better.

Increasing Risk	
When to	**How to**
• Innovation activities	• Name it — acknowledge the risk.
• People ready to stretch outside their comfort zone	• Highlight the rewards of risk-taking.
• Old way isn't working	• Initiate new topics of conversation.
• Implementing a change	• Break routines.
• Perceived cost/loss	• Raise the stakes.
	• Bring new voices into the conversation.

Chapter Takeaways

- Know when to create an environment of safety and when to gently push people out of their comfort zones for growth.

- To enhance safety, ensure people feel valued and connected. It's our responsibility to address any exclusionary or inappropriate behavior that undermines safety.

- Understand how others perceive risk — what seems high-stakes or uncomfortable for some, others might embrace with ease, and vice versa.

- People must feel that you understand and empathize with their concerns before they are receptive to ways to reduce risk.

- Skilled facilitators balance risk and safety by understanding their comfort level in relation to others and choose from a range of options to achieve their goals.

11 Support Development

Provide insights and opportunities for individual
and group growth.

I create the conditions that encourage people to accept my support.

I guide people in reflecting on their own behaviors.

I offer specific, timely feedback that includes the impact.

I help individuals and teams reach their potential

Ken found himself teetering on the edge of a pivotal sale. He knew he needed an extra boost of credibility to seal the deal, and who better than Nadia, the design architect? Ken was certain that Nadia's presence in the meeting would work wonders.

His confidence quickly gave way to dismay as the meeting began to unravel. Nadia, in an unexpected twist, started reciting slides verbatim and got lost in a labyrinth of technical jargon. The customer's face bore unmistakable signs of confusion, and Ken had no choice but to interject and steer the conversation back on track.

The puzzle of what had gone wrong gnawed at him, and his admiration for Nadia made confronting the issue all the more daunting. Tempted to chalk up her behavior as a mere hiccup or an off day, he hesitated to discuss it with her. After all, he didn't want to make things worse.

The conversation that desperately had to happen was shelved, buried beneath unspoken words. The feedback that might have helped Nadia was left unsaid. Ken decided to go solo after that, excluding her from subsequent customer meetings, hoping to minimize the risk of a repeat performance.

Moments like the one Ken and Nadia experienced can catalyze withdrawal and angst. In skillful hands, though, such moments can also bring real gifts: They become opportunities to nurture growth and development.

Support Development can take many forms, from more prescriptive interventions to less directive choices. The key lies in choosing the approach that best fits the individual or group and serves the desired outcome.

Support Options	Instruct Tell or show "how to"	Give Feedback Help others understand their strengths and/ or development areas.	Coach Empower others to develop their own insights, solutions, and strategies.
When to	• The individual or group is: • Seeking new knowledge or skill. • Unable to solve it themselves	• The individual or group is: • Open to feedback • Demonstrating a behavior that's hindering or supporting their success.	• The individual or group is: • Able to take ownership for their development. • Capable of finding their own solutions.
Examples	• Teaching a peer how to solve a problem • Telling a group how to complete a task	• Offering an observation on a behavior and the impact. • Leading a debrief session on lessons learned after a product launch.	• Helping an individual explore ways to connect with their audience better. • Leading a discussion to help a group improve their performance.

Instructing falls on the more directive end of the continuum because it's giving specific instructions on how to perform tasks or develop specific skills. For instance, we are often sought out to work with senior leadership teams who want to become more high-performing. In that situation, they look to us to teach them how to lead group decision-making approaches.

Giving feedback falls in the middle of the continuum, striking a balance between directive and less directive approaches. Take the story of Ken and Nadia. That was a situation where Ken could have offered support to Nadia by giving her feedback about how she showed up in the meeting. In a group setting, the meeting leader might give feedback to the group about how they are working together. They might say, "I noticed how respectful you were in listening to each other's opinions, even when you disagreed. As a result, you came to a decision that everyone can support."

Coaching is even less directive. It empowers people collaboratively to develop their own insights, solutions, and strategies. The hallmark of coaching is asking thought-provoking questions, actively listening, and guiding people to uncover their own path.

A meeting leader might coach by asking curious questions and encouraging team members to explore different perspectives. They might ask, "What are some alternative approaches we could consider for this challenge?" or "How do you think we can leverage the data to achieve our goal?"

In this chapter, we'll focus on approaches for giving feedback and coaching. They offer the biggest bang for the buck and tend to be where most people want to improve when supporting others.

Create the Conditions for People to Accept Your Support

The starting point is to be clear and honest with yourself about your intentions.

 Is your motivation to help your audience improve or grow versus fixing a clash with your personal preference or style?

 Do you have enough knowledge and understanding of their situation?

 Can your audience act upon it? Is the situation in their control?

 Do they perceive you as an ally and not an adversary?

If the answer to those questions is "not quite," ask yourself, *Am I the right person to be supporting them?* If not, consider who else might be better positioned to help them.

We know a leader who schedules a five-minute debrief call immediately after important account management calls. She intentionally creates an environment to support people's development by making it safe to not be perfect. She does that by inviting the team to give *her* feedback first. She starts with a question like, "How did I do at addressing that curveball question?" or "Could I have done anything differently?" By modeling her openness to receive input and even assessing her own performance first, she makes it safe for others to be more open to doing the same.

Here are some practical ways to make it easier to support people's development.

Create the Conditions to Support People's Development	
Normalize Development Conversations	**It Sounds Like ...**
Model Self-Awareness Give yourself feedback in front of others.	"I know I get long-winded when I get a question. I'm trying to be more succinct when I get nervous."
Invite Balanced Feedback Show openness to receiving feedback.	"When the call ends, tell me what worked well and what I could do better."
Demonstrate Your Interest in Supporting Them Assess their receptiveness.	"I remember what it was like to lead those cross-functional team meetings. It's not easy. Now that you're the meeting leader, would you like support from me during or after the meetings?" If they say yes, ask this: 'Is there anything in particular that you'd like feedback on later?'"

Assess Their Receptivity

Imagine a friend struggling to assemble a complex puzzle. You witness their frustration as they attempt to force-fit the pieces together, and you know they could benefit from your puzzle-solving experience — but when you offer to lend a hand, your friend declines your help. They insist on tackling the puzzle on their own. Just like in real life, and especially if you've ever parented a teenager, sometimes people don't want to accept your support, even when it comes from a well-meaning place. It could be due to their independence or pride, or simply not feeling ready to address the need.

The opposite can often be true, too. We hesitate to offer support, convinced people neither want nor require our help. We question our own credentials, thinking, *Who am I to help when I'm no expert?* It's especially true when working with clients, peers, or more-senior people.

It's worth remembering that we're not alone in our struggles. Sometimes, offering a helping hand can be the very thing that untangles our own doubts and brings us closer to understanding ourselves and others.

Manage Your Self-Talk to Support People's Development	
Unsupportive	**Supportive**
• It's not my place to say anything. I'm not their boss.	• I care about their success and they deserve to know how they are being perceived.
• They aren't going to like what I have to say.	• If they know my intentions are good, they are more likely to accept my help.
• They already know they do a good job.	• I want them to feel appreciated and not taken for granted.

How do you gauge someone's receptivity to your help?

First, consider their level of self-awareness. Do they have a realistic and clear understanding of their own abilities and limitations? Self-aware people embrace their strengths while acknowledging their weaknesses without falling into self-deprecation or denial.

Then, observe the signs. Watch their reactions and body language when you offer help. Are their eyes wide open, eager for more of your insights, or are they dismissive? Are they open to different perspectives, even if they don't fully agree? Do they appreciate your help?

Last, consider what you know about the person and your relationship. Once again, test your motives for offering support. What trigger might you flip if you're not careful?

If they aren't receptive to your support, work on setting the foundation for a more trusting relationship. Encourage them to share their insights and challenges by listening actively. Visit the "Listen" chapter for more on building trust and understanding.

If they are open to your support, you have many choices for how to help them.

Instruct

Imagine using complicated software. For the IT pro, it's like gliding effortlessly, but for a newbie, it's like riding a bike for the first time: lots of wobbling and a few crashes. The expert might forget the early wobbles, while the beginner is just trying not end up with a permanent bruise. When the best way to support someone's development is through teaching, keep a few things in mind.

Understand their starting point: Before diving into instruction, take the time to understand the individual's current knowledge, skills, and experience related to the subject matter. Ask open-ended questions to gauge their understanding and identify any misconceptions or knowledge gaps. Tailor your approach based on this initial assessment to ensure that you start from a point that is relevant and comprehensible to them.

Simplify complex concepts: You might be well-versed in intricate details and advanced concepts. However, when supporting someone who is new to the topic, deconstruct complex ideas into easily digestible, manageable parts. Use everyday language, relatable analogies, and visual aids to help them grasp the basics. Visit the chapter about "Subject Matter and Suit Context" for more.

Make learning interactive: Actively involve the person by encouraging questions, discussions, and hands-on practice. Then create opportunities for them to apply the knowledge and skills, providing constructive feedback and coaching along the way. (More about that later!) Engaging in active learning not only solidifies their understanding; it also boosts their confidence and motivation to continue learning and improving.

Give Feedback

Giving feedback can feel as nerve-racking as getting it, because it involves potential discomfort, uncertainty, and the fear of negatively affecting the relationship between the giver and receiver. This shared vulnerability underscores the importance of establishing a safe and supportive environment for feedback conversations.

There are plenty of feedback methods out there, each with its own strengths. What unites them all is the emphasis on meaningful conversations rather than mere checkboxes.

We've crafted a framework to facilitate constructive and easily digestible feedback delivery. Here's a tool designed to help you provide feedback that's both valuable and well-received.

The CHOICE Feedback Framework

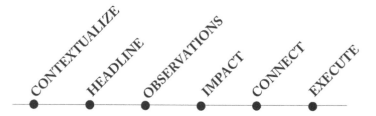

Contextualize

A surefire way to strike anxiety and fear in someone is to jump in with no preamble, "Hey, can I give you some feedback?" As David Rock, author of *Your Brain at Work*, wrote, "Feedback creates a strong threat response in the brain. People are hyper-sensitive to anything that feeds their 'negativity bias' — the tendency to react defensively to anything the brain views as a threat."[70]

One of the simplest ways to build trust and buy-in is by stating your intentions.[71] When you clarify and confirm the purpose of the conversation, people are less likely to blame you for the message you convey. For instance, "You said you wanted to work on executive presence and 'owning the room.' Let's talk about how you showed up in the meeting" is an upfront declaration. When it's genuine, it acts as a shield against defensiveness and leads the recipient to be more receptive to your message. If you don't have a strong, trusting relationship and someone isn't accustomed to debriefing after a meeting, for instance, stating your intention will help them feel more oriented and less resistant to the conversation.

70 Rock, D. (2009). *Your Brain at Work: Strategies for Overcoming Distraction, Regaining Focus, and Working Smarter All Day Long*. Harper Business.
71 John, Leslie, Blunden, Hayley, and Liu, Heidi. (2019). "Shooting the Messenger." *Journal of Experimental Psychology:General* Volume148:Number 4: 644–666.

Evan was on a video call with his peer, Lucia, and the client, Madeline. Lucia pushed back on a deadline that was previously agreed upon. Her phrasing was matter-of-fact yet harsh. Internally, Evan cringed and Lucia didn't pick up on how Madeline's body language telegraphed her anger.

The next day, Evan and Lucia had a follow-up call to discuss action items from the meeting.

Before offering your point of view, invite the person's perspective first and then listen. Be curious and guide them to reflect on their behavior. For example, you might ask, "What do you think went well in the meeting and what would you want to change?" There are many reasons to listen first before offering your feedback.

 You may not have all the facts or are misinterpreting what happened.

 It signals that you value their input and respect their viewpoint.

 It builds the person's self-awareness when prompted to reflect on their behaviors.

 They may give themselves the feedback (and you don't have to).

As they offer their point of view, listen and verbalize your understanding of what you're hearing — *even if you don't agree*. For individuals to be open and receptive to your feedback, they must feel heard and understood.

Evan: "How do you think that meeting went with Madeline?"

Lucia: "I think it went as well as it possibly could. I'm glad she now understands the timeline isn't reasonable, so there's no confusion. I'm tired of her taking advantage of us."

Evan (restatement): "You wanted to reset her expectations."

Lucia: "Exactly. We should have renegotiated the deadline months ago, when she asked for all those changes."

Headline, Observations, Impact

Once you have communicated your goals in offering feedback and heard from others, it's time to share feedback in a clear, specific, and focused way. The Headline-Observations-Impact section of the CHOICE framework constitutes the feedback itself.

Headline: Start by framing the feedback in a bite-sized way. A headline summarizes the feedback so the details to follow are focused and clear. Not only does formulating a headline help the recipient understand and retain your feedback, it helps you start on track.

Evan to Lucia: "I think that the way you expressed your opinion upset Madeline and undermined our ability to renegotiate."

Observations: Receiving feedback without behavioral specifics is like trying to navigate a maze in the dark without a flashlight. You know there's something there, but you can't quite see where you're going, and it's easy to get lost along the way. Offering specific, observable behaviors cuts down on any confusion and helps the person receiving feedback to see more clearly.

Being more specific means being more factual. It's hard because our brain often jumps to judgments first.[72] To be on solid ground with feedback, you must be able to identify the objective behaviors that give rise to your opinions or judgments. When you notice a behavior and want to give feedback, play the moment in your mind again and ask yourself what, specifically, was happening.

Imagine you are a video camera and do a "camera check." What could actually be seen and heard? A video camera wouldn't show someone being aloof in a meeting, but it would capture crossed arms, looking down, and no talking. The behavior is what you want to address.

Evan to Lucia: "You said in a loud tone of voice, 'There's no way we can do that.' Then you crossed your arms and rolled your eyes. Did you notice how Madeline's behavior changed in response?"

Think about an opinion or judgment you have about a recent interaction. Can you identify the observable behaviors to be addressed? Here are some examples.

---

72 Kahneman, D., Slovic, P., and Tversky, A. (1982). *Judgment Under Uncertainty: Heuristics and Biases.* Cambridge University Press.

	The Interpretation	Give Behavioral Specifics
Corrective	Rude	"In the team meeting, you kept your camera off when everyone else had their cameras on. You stayed on mute and didn't contribute to the discussion."
	Not Confident	"Frequently, you touched your face, twirled your pen, and said, 'I might be wrong but …'"
	Not Taking Charge	"You knew the answer, but remained silent and looked at me when the senior leader asked you a direct question."
Positive	Team Player	"When the client gave you that compliment, you were quick to point out that Joe and Nick were big contributors, too."
	Problem-Solver	"When the team began to complain about the situation, you stayed calm and started to offer alternatives."
	Strategic	"In the meeting, you reminded us to stay focused on the bigger picture, and it prevented us from getting too caught up in details."

Impact: The last element of well-articulated feedback is naming impact. As one of Kat's mentors, Cal Sutliff, used to say, "The measure of good feedback is, 'Is it valuable to the recipient?'" Articulating the impact of behaviors grounds your feedback in that value. If the impact is missing from a corrective feedback message, you often won't see a change in behavior. *So what?* a recipient might think.

Evan to Lucia: "As soon as you responded this way, Madeline said that we're breaking our agreement. The conversation ended there and now it's going to get escalated. The impact is that she views us as a roadblock and not a partner."

Connect

The conversation doesn't stop with delivering the message. Give the receiver an opportunity to process it. No matter how well you set the context and offer feedback with the impact, people often need time to reflect, replay the situation, ask questions, and share their opinions.

In the book *Thanks for the Feedback: The Science and Art of Receiving Feedback Well*,[73] Douglas Stone and Sheila Heen note three types of feedback triggers that can block the capacity to receive comments and ideas:

 Truth triggers: feeling like the feedback is untrue or unhelpful

 Relationship triggers: resisting who the feedback is coming from

 Identity triggers: a sense that whether true or not, the feedback is just too threatening to hear

Recognizing the type of triggers can help us navigate another's reactions. It is unrealistic to expect that feedback will always be received wholly and completely at first. Expect people to dismiss positive feedback or express confusion or resistance to corrective feedback, no matter how successfully you executed the previous steps.

In this phase of the feedback conversations, your goals are to answer questions, clarify any confusion about your Headline-Observations-Impact message, and field reactions. Once the feedback recipient has shared

73 Stone, Douglas, and Heen, Sheila (2015). *Thanks for the Feedback: The Science and Art of Receiving Feedback Well*. Penguin (pp. 16–17).

their reactions and you both feel aligned in terms of understanding the message and what feels valuable to the recipient, you can move on to the final stage of the CHOICE process.

Lucia: "I know I lost my temper. It's just that we're so understaffed and she underestimates what it will take to meet deadlines. Plus, I don't feel like the account manager ever defends us and doesn't ever push back on unreasonable requests, so I felt I had to for the sake of my team that's already burned out."

Evan: "You feel like you're at a breaking point."

Lucia: "Yes, but I know I shouldn't take it out on the client. I really need to set clear boundaries with the account manager."

Execute

Feedback is valuable when it helps to modify or reinforce future behavior. Positive feedback motivates the receiver to repeat the behavior more consciously, while corrective feedback is about changing behavior.

If the feedback requires something to be addressed and fixed, help create a plan to get things back on track. Asking the receiver for their ideas and thoughts first, even if you have recommendations to offer, can reinforce their accountability and commitment.

Lucia: "Do you think I should send Madeline an email to apologize?"

Evan: "I think a follow-up would be good. How do you decide when to send something by email instead of picking up the phone and having a conversation? I know I can misinterpret tone and intention when I read an email, so when in doubt, I usually try to talk live to the person."

Lucia: "I should probably call her."

Evan: "It also seems like you need to schedule a meeting with the account manager to work out the bigger issue between you two."

Lucia: "I'm not looking forward to it, but you're right. It's overdue."

Try This: Give Feedback

Contextualize Provide background or framing, state your intention, and invite their point of view. *"You wanted to ensure everyone is actively participating in the meeting.* *What are you noticing? How do you think it's going?"*	
Headline Summarize the key message. *"Your participation is influencing the level of honesty and candor among people in the meeting."*	
Observations and Impact Offer "camera-check" observable behaviors, including the impact. *"Whenever there's silence after I ask a question, you are the first to answer. Then, people agree without offering their own perspective. It's inhibiting the participation and interaction you want."*	
Connect Discuss the feedback. Ask open-ended questions to bring reactions and feelings to the surface. Explore ways to shift the behavior to be more successful. *"What's your reaction to that?"* *"What could you do (or not do) to create a safer space for people to speak up?"*	
Execute Support an action plan. Help the receiver plan next steps and follow up. *"Wait to offer your opinion until at least three others speak up first. Let's check in at the next break to see if that's having the result you want."*	

Giving Feedback to Groups

While the process above applies in group settings, there are some extra considerations.

Get a group agreement that you'll give them feedback. Just as with individuals, you want to have buy-in to receiving feedback before diving in. Although in some situations, like formal training, the power of the facilitator to give feedback is implied, it cannot hurt to have explicit agreements about how and when feedback will be given. In the "Serve the Purpose" chapter, we outline how to make group agreements that enable you to give feedback without catching the group off guard.

Encourage the group to assess their own and peer performance. Create moments for the group to discuss their own performance, identifying strengths and areas for improvement. This fosters the team to own their development. A great time for feedback is during a debrief. Consider questions such as:

 How do you think you worked as a team during this phase of the project?

 What worked or didn't work in how you interacted?

 How could the team improve for the next phase?

Give feedback about the process, not the person. Save individual feedback for private, one-on-one moments. When it's time to give feedback to the group, focus on the process. For instance, Therese was leading a meeting with a senior team and observed that the group was going round and round on a topic but making little progress. She pointed it out by saying, "I'm noticing a pattern in how you're approaching the topic. You seem to be focused on the symptoms and not the root cause." Because she gave feedback to the group in this way, no individual felt called out or attacked.

A Note on Positive Feedback

Even though we have mentioned both positive and corrective feedback already, we believe it bears highlighting that positive feedback can be one of the most effective developmental tools. Catching and acknowledging people doing things well provides a highly efficient way to bolster future behavior. Especially when people are burned out or undervalued, a positive, behavioral feedback message can act like filling an empty gas tank.

Positive feedback recharges people and encourages growth. If you are the type who thinks, "My boss or client doesn't need positive feedback from me" or "I'm not thanking people for doing their job," think again! Positive recognition can be a great motivator, along with enhancing the receiver's perception of the person giving the positive message.[74]

When we work with groups, we demonstrate the power of positive feedback as a learning tool through

74 Svetieva, E. and Lopes, P.N. (2022). "The What and How of Positive Feedback: A Review and Experimental Study of Positive Feedback "Best Practices"; Humphrey, R.H., Ashkanasy, N.M., and Troth, A.C. (Ed.). (Year). Emotions and Negativity (*Research on Emotion in Organizations*, Vol. 17), Emerald Publishing Limited, Bingley, pp. 251–274. https://doi.org/10.1108/S1746-979120210000017018.

the improvisational activity called the Dolphin Game. Dolphins, like most mammals, learn fastest through positive reinforcement. When a dolphin exhibits the desired behavior, the trainer throws them a fish and the dolphin learns to repeat that behavior. In a workshop setting, one person (the dolphin) leaves the room and the remaining group collectively decides on an action to get the person to accomplish. It could be any behavior, such as write their name on a whiteboard, do a push-up, sit in a certain chair.

When the dolphin returns to the room, the group offers only nonverbal signals, like the sound of "ding" as a way to reinforce any behavior, no matter how small, in the direction of the chosen action. In our experience, it takes our dolphin less than three minutes to achieve the desired behavior. That's it!

We're not advocating the sandwich approach to feed-back, which is starting with a positive message, zinging someone with corrective feedback, and then smoothing everything over with a final positive message. It might sound like, "The client really sees you as an expert, but you talked too fast during your presentation. But it's probably not a big deal. You're great!" It sounds disingenuous and people are most likely to misinterpret the message.

Coaching

Feedback is the right tool when the emphasis is on what just happened. It's primarily retrospective and it helps by providing specific guidance and correcting or acknowledging behaviors.

Coaching focuses on growth and development. It's the best way to support people in exploring possibilities and setting goals.

A coach's job is to help unlock potential — to help someone become more capable in a particular area and to make a lasting improvement versus finding a solution to today's issue. A coach doesn't push a person into something. Rather, they help the person clarify what is right for them.

Great coaching doesn't happen by accident. It's a skill. Professional coaches and facilitators spend their careers developing their capabilities and approach, and there are many methodologies, models, and certification programs out there. For our purposes, we'll focus on how to have a coaching conversation to support a person's development.

Effective Coaching Conversations

A good coach has a way of leading a conversation that focuses on long-term development versus a short-term, problem-solving conversation. The conversation has structure to it. The four steps that frame an effective coaching conversation are purpose, assessment, choice, and execution (PACE).

Purpose

The starting point for coaching is determining the Purpose and goal. You're exploring the coachee's values and motivations. This phase involves deep self-reflection and exploration to define what truly matters to the coachee and what they want to achieve.

Since the heart of coaching is asking questions, here are the types of questions to ask during this stage. (Not all questions will be useful for all situations. Use only the ones that seem helpful, and in your own words.)

 What do you want or need to achieve? What, specifically, does that include?

 What are your core values and beliefs when it comes to this goal?

 What's motivating you to take action?

 What does success look like to you?

Assessment

Once the purpose is established, the coaching process moves into the Assessment phase. Here, the coach and coachee examine the current situation, strengths, weaknesses, opportunities, and challenges. This phase provides a comprehensive understanding of the coachee's starting point.

Let's imagine a data scientist whose goal is to get promoted to a director level. They've been passed over in the past because of poor communication skills with their peers and cross-functional teams. This phase of the coaching process involves uncovering the factors that have to be addressed for the coachee. Some questions to draw them out may be:

 What feedback have you received from others regarding this goal?

 What are your strengths that can help you in achieving this goal?

 What do you need to learn or develop to get the results you want?

 What are the main obstacles or challenges you're facing in pursuit of your goal?

 What limiting beliefs or self-doubts might be holding you back?

Choice

In the Choice phase, the focus is on helping the coachee explore and evaluate various development options and strategies to achieve their goals, considering their skills, values, preferences, and resources. For our data scientist, the development step might be how to tailor their messages to a less-technical audience or how to address conflicts more constructively in meetings.

Questions that work at this phase include:

 What are some potential paths or strategies you've considered to achieve your goal?

How do you like to learn? (Examples might be reading books, on-the-job experiences, mentoring.)

 What obstacles might you encounter?

 What could you do to get around the obstacles?

 Of all the options, what's most compelling?

 If you did that, would that give you the results you want?

 What resources and support do you need?

Execution

You can't force a person to grow, even when you see their potential. The person must be motivated to treat their development plan as a priority. In this step, you support the coachee in developing a concrete action plan that they will own. The coach provides support, accountability, and guidance. Ask questions that invite the coachee to take ownership:

 What are you going to do and by when?

 What will you have achieved by our next meeting?

 When (what date and time) should we meet next about this?

 What support do you need from me?

In more formal coaching relationships, the coach might be committing to something, too. For instance, you might offer to give them feedback. If you're taking on some responsibility, this is the time to confirm your commitment, too.

Try This: Plan for a Coaching Conversation Using PACE

Purpose Identify and clarify the coachee's purpose and goals.	
Assessment Get a clear picture of the coachee's reality relative to their goal (such as strengths, weaknesses, obstacles, opportunities).	
Choice Explore options and strategies for achieving the goal.	
Execution Develop an action plan owned by the coachee. Provide support, accountability, and guidance.	

Of all the facilitator contributions, "Support People's Development" can often be the most rewarding one for you. Through feedback and coaching, you get a front-row seat to watch people and teams transform. There's an incredible sense of fulfillment in helping people flourish, which serves as a reminder of the meaningful impact you can have on the lives and careers of others.

Chapter Takeaways

- Choose the development approach that best fits your specific participants and serves the desired outcome.

- Assess your intentions. Are you motivated to help the person or group grow, or are you trying to impose your personal preference? Ensure you have enough knowledge of their situation to offer valuable support.

- When instructing, take into consideration current knowledge and experience and tailor your approach accordingly. Simplify complex concepts. Make the learning process interactive.

- When giving feedback, use the CHOICE Feedback Framework: Contextualize, Headline, Observations, Impact, Connect, and Execute, to facilitate a constructive conversation.

- Coach using the PACE framework — Purpose, Assessment, Choice, and Execution. The Purpose phase involves exploring values and motivations; the Assessment phase delves into the current situation and challenges; the Choice phase focuses on development options and strategies; and the Execution phase supports the coachee in creating and owning a concrete action plan, emphasizing motivation and accountability.

12 Putting it All Together

Phew — that was a lot, eh? Having consumed what might feel like an overwhelming number of tips and tools, you may be asking how you can actually start to apply them in practice in context. Worry not! We have your back.

Remember: You need not master all of these skills all at once to up your leadership and communication game. Strategically focus on one or two contributions at a time, either because the context calls for them, or because you want to expand your performance range.

Here are a few ways to engage with the contributions to maximize your development and impact.

1. Review the assessment in Chapter 1. Identify a contribution that you would especially like to improve.

And/or ...

2. Pinpoint a specific situation in which you would like to have impact.

3. Use this template to prepare to engage your new behaviors.

Facilitation Advantage Application Plan

1. Situation: What is the context in which you want to apply your facilitation skills (e.g., team meeting, 1:1 sales call, problem-solving session)?

    _____

    _____

2. Facilitation Goal: What is *one* way you would like to have an impact with your facilitation skills (increase engagement, support innovation, resolve contention, build a new relationship)?

    _____

    _____

3. Facilitation Challenge: What current dynamics do you want to address (one participant dominates discussion; participants look to you to lead all discussions; we are unfocused; we do not know each other)?

    _____

    _____

4. Action Plan: Choose a contribution and specific behaviors to try and identify how you will measure success.

    _____

    _____

Here is an example.

Facilitation Advantage Application Plan

1. Situation: What is the context in which you want to apply your facilitation skills (e.g., team meeting, 1:1 sales call, problem-solving session)?

    Facilitating a team offsite

2. Facilitation Goal: What is *one* way you would like to have impact with your facilitation skills (increase engagement, support innovation, resolve contention, build a new relationship)?

    Increase a sense of inclusion among team members

3. Facilitation Challenge: What current dynamics do you want to address (one participant dominates discussion; participants look to you to lead all discussions; we are unfocused; we do not know each other)?

    I tend to lead conversations and be deferred to

4. Action Plan:

Contribution	Behavior(s)	Measure of Success
Listen	Restate to clarify and confirm understanding beyond facts and data.	Participants say, "Yes, that's right!" Participants add more to initial statements. Participants share new thoughts, ideas, and feelings.
Establish Presence	Raise others' status by sitting rather than standing Asking questions Pausing to leave space for others Inviting expertise from the room	Others talk more than I do. More participants share. Participants demonstrate open body language and take space.

Questions and Answers

Over the years, leaders will approach us with questions that tend to be common and resonate with others. Here are some clear and practical answers to help you navigate the sticky situations you may find yourself in as a facilitator. These common questions are a testament to the shared experiences of leaders at all levels. As you think about where to apply your new skills, take a look at the situations below for inspiration and answers.

1. How do I get people to speak up?

People are more motivated to speak up when you are attentive and genuinely interested in what they have to say. Avoid distractions, make eye contact, and turn your body toward the speaker to signal you are ready to listen.

Next, ask better questions. Instead of asking "Any questions?," offer a more curious, open-ended question, like, "There's no right or wrong to this question, how do you see this working?"

Finally, try pausing more. Create space for people to think and then respond. Talking without pausing encourages people to stay silent. Visit Chapter 8 about listening for more.

2. How do I manage moments when I'm caught off-guard?

No one can be prepared for every possible scenario. When the unexpected happens and your heart races, take a deep breath before responding. Breathing helps you manage your outward reaction and provides the necessary moment to compose yourself. Then, verify your understanding instead of jumping to conclusions, especially when thrown off by a question or comment. Verbalize what you heard to check your assumptions. Read how to restate in Chapter 8.

Last, respond concisely. Overexplaining lessens your credibility and invites more doubts and more questions. Answer honestly but briefly, when possible.

3. What's the best way to deliver a tough message?

Whether you're a rip the Band-aid off type or prefer a gentler approach, start by stepping in the shoes of the impacted audience. Think about how the news will affect them and what they will want to know. Then use that insight to craft the message.

Tough messages are made even harder when the deliverer doesn't get to the point quickly. Practice delivering the message aloud. You're likely to be nervous when the moment arrives; practicing helps you refine your message and delivery.

Last, listen with empathy. People want to feel acknowledged and understood. Verbalize what you're hearing, including feelings, even if you disagree with their point of view. Avoid justifying the decision or encouraging people to look on the bright side. What most of us want are clarity, conciseness, and acknowledgment of the impact on us. Find more about listening with empathy in Chapter 8 ("Listen") and Chapter 10 ("Balance Risk and Safety").

4. How do I keep people's attention?

It's somewhat of a myth that people have short attention spans. They'll binge-watch a ten-episode show on Netflix or stay up until 3:00 a.m. to read a good book. People reserve their attention for high-value content and experiences. Keeping people's attention starts *before* you are with them. Find out what matters most to them or the problem they are trying to solve. Then, tailor the content so it resonates with them. Check out Chapter 4 ("Share Subject-Matter Knowledge") and Chapter 5 ("Suit Context") for more.

Telling a story is another way to keep people engaged. Imagine you need to deliver data about security training to a group of sales leaders and you're worried it will be a snooze fest. You could tell a story of a security breach that affected a customer or a time when a wise salesperson saved the day by spotting a hacking attempt. Find out more in Chapter 7 ("Engage with Story").

Sometimes we notice people trying to power through an agenda instead of pausing to notice what the group needs. When you catch people's eyes getting droopy or you feel the energy draining, mix things up. Take a break, start a conversation, or change what you're doing. Find more in the Chapter 8.

5. One person keeps dominating the conversation. How do I rebalance the interaction?

The over-sharer, the boaster, or the person who just loves the sound of their own voice can derail a meeting, but there are some practical ways to manage the moment. First, the aim isn't to stifle the person, but rather to create space for others to contribute.

When a person drones on and on, restate their point. Often, when people feel they are being heard and understood, they no longer feel the need to repeat themselves. And here's a little secret: Usually no one gets offended if you interrupt them to restate your understanding of their perspective. To do it well, match their energy and say something like, "Ooh, wait a second! Let me see if I'm catching your main point. Is it …?"

Be the crossing guard by directing conversational traffic. Try saying, "Sven, it looks like Mary has something to say about that. Mary, what are you thinking?" or "Let's hear from someone who hasn't spoken up yet," or "Sven, we have just another minute left." Another subtle approach is not to give full attention to the over-sharer. Break eye contact and look at others, for example.

A final option is to have a feedback conversation with the person. They may not be aware of the impact of their behavior. Find more ideas in Chapter 11 ("Support People's Development").

6. How do I present effectively to people who have more expertise or experience than I have?

Experts appreciate sharing what they know, so use it and acknowledge the wisdom in the room. Invite them to contribute by asking a question like, "There are more than fifty years of collective experience in oncology here. What's your best advice for someone who's new to the department?"

Be aware of a status dynamic at play in these moments. Chapter 6 ("Establish Presence") offers behavioral tips about what to do to create a connection when the field is uneven.

7. How do I prevent a meeting from going off-track?

Before the meeting, send an agenda, including the purpose, why it's important (from the attendee's perspective), and the desired outcomes.

In the meeting, offer ground rules and treat them like an agreement versus an expectation. Anticipate where the group might go off-track and discuss how you'll keep the guard rails up during the meeting.

Listen for early off-track signals before they derail the meeting and then call it out. For instance, "Right now, we are focused on what to do for the Southwest market, not the Northeast" or "We had ten minutes on the agenda for this topic and we've spent fifteen minutes."

Renegotiate with the group when the meeting is off-track. Acknowledge what's happening and get agreement about how to adjust the timing or take topics off-line. Check out Chapter 9 ("Serve the Purpose").

8. When a senior person attends our meeting, everyone defers to them. How do I even the playing field?

In the Chapter 5, "Establish Presence," we write about status dynamics and that the aim is to create status parity, where connection and collaboration are enabled. Try talking to the senior person. In our work with thousands of senior executives, we have found that they are often frustrated when people defer to them first, preferring to hear new ideas and not influence thinking prematurely. If that's the case for you, recommend that the senior person speak last or mention it directly to the group like, "Mike is here to listen to your ideas first."

Pay attention to psychological safety, which we explore in the Chapter 10 ("Balance Risk and Safety"). No one will speak up if they think their ideas will be judged or shot down by the senior leader. If safety is low, consider having a conversation with that leader and offer ways to make it easier for people to speak up first.

9. How do I make the most of hybrid meetings when a mix of people are in person and virtual?

According to Microsoft's Work Trend Index, 43 percent of remote workers say they don't feel included in meetings. Start by upping your technology game. Make it easier for virtual attendees to hear and see what's happening.

A discussion will often default to the people who are face to face, leaving virtual attendees feeling excluded. Give equal priority to remote participants by inviting them to talk first or ensuring they get equal air time.

10. I'm the sixth presenter in a day-long meeting and my time slot is after lunch. How can I stand out and be memorable?

Forget serving a big pot of coffee! Boost the energy and fight against fatigue by telling a story. In Chapter 7 ("Engage with Story"), we offer how to craft a story that grabs people's attention and makes your message memorable.

Another way to break from the path paved by previous presenters is to shift how you engage with the group. Vary your voice, tone, speed, and inflection to keep people's attention. Prompt a conversation instead of speaking to or reading from slides. If you can get the group talking instead of passively listening to you, you'll awaken their interest and boost their energy level.

11. How can I break my habit of using filler words such as *Um*, *Like*, and *You Know*?

Filler words are normal and it's not always something that needs fixing. Filler words can even play an important role in communicating effectively — they can subtly convey emotions ("This news is, uh, difficult for all of us").

However, if filler words become excessive or hinder your confidence or credibility, they're worth addressing. To avoid the verbal crutch, become more consciously aware of the behavior, when it happens, and what might be causing it. Record yourself speaking to identify the pattern. If you notice fillers at the end of a sentence, try pausing to take a breath and slow down.

12. My thirty-minute time slot just shrank to ten minutes. What do I do?

Avoid the mistake of talking faster in an attempt to cram everything into a shorter timeframe. Rushing through your content is likely to confuse people and give the impression that you're not in control.

Instead, start by distilling your message to the essence. What's the one thing you want the audience to know or do? Share the rest in an email or follow up with people later. Another option is to ask the group for their input about what's most important: "I'm conscious of our tight agenda. What's most important for you to know right now?" They'll appreciate the consideration and you'll demonstrate the ability to pivot quickly. Visit Chapter 9 ("Serve the Purpose") for more ideas.

13. What's the best way to manage my nerves before a high-stakes moment?

Nerves are our body's way of telling us something is important and meaningful to us; otherwise, we wouldn't be nervous, right? Try shifting from a mindset of "I'm afraid I'm going to fail" to "I'm excited I get to try something new."

Several experiments conducted at the Harvard Business School by Allison Woods Brooks found that how you interpret your emotions makes a difference. She wrote,

"People have a very strong intuition that trying to calm down is the best way to cope with their anxiety, but that can be very difficult and ineffective. When people feel anxious and try to calm down, they are thinking about all the things that could go badly. When they are excited, they are thinking about how things could go well."

Chapter 2 ("Manage Yourself") offers a host of ideas about how to support yourself to show up as calm and confident.

14. How can I get more comfortable with eye contact?

Eye contact is a source of anxiety for a lot of people, and it can be tricky. Give too much eye contact and it feels like staring; not enough and you risk appearing not confident, disconnected, or, worse, untrustworthy.

Think of receiving eye contact instead of giving it. When people make eye contact with you, meet their gaze. And you don't have to do it all the time. In North American cultures, a good rule of thumb is to maintain eye contact 50 percent of the time while talking and 70 percent of the time while listening. When you make eye contact, hold it for four to five seconds before slowly diverting your gaze. If you have a friend in the meeting, begin by making eye contact with them to get comfortable, then shift your eyes to others.

In some cultures, eye contact can be perceived as rude or disrespectful. Be aware of the cultural norms where you're interacting.

15. I want to read the room better. Where do I start?

You are thirty minutes into an hour-long virtual project status meeting with three members of the client team. One person stoically looks straight ahead. Another slowly rubs their temples with their eyes closed. You see the side profile of the third person, who props his head up with his hand and is apparently looking at a different screen. Are you noticing it?

Reading the room requires you to scan the emotional landscape around you and then respond to what you're noticing. It starts with becoming more observant and paying attention to verbal and nonverbal behaviors. Don't assume you know what's driving those behaviors. In the scenario just described, maybe the clients are processing what it will mean to implement the new software, or maybe they are confused or bored because you aren't addressing their needs.

When you begin to pick up on behaviors, stay curious. If you notice people looking at their watches, you might say, "I'm conscious of everyone's time. What level of detail would you like me to go into?" If you notice people remaining quiet, yet stealing glances at one another, you might say, "I'm getting a sense that there's something underlying your silence. What am I missing?"

Keep honing your ability to observe and interpret group behaviors when you're not in the hot seat. You'll have more mental bandwidth when all eyes aren't on you. Reading the room is a form of listening. Find out more in Chapter 8.

16. Some of my team members are afraid to speak up in meetings. What can I do?

Get curious about what's driving their hesitancy. Do people feel their ideas won't be heard? Are they afraid of making a mistake? When people experience their team members as open-minded and accepting of different points of view, and vulnerability is viewed as a strength and not a weakness, they speak up.

In Chapter 10 ("Balance Risk and Safety"), we write about psychological safety as the lynchpin to team performance. To increase safety, lower the stakes of the conversation. It might sound like, "Let's get all ideas on the table. Everyone's opinions count. We're not judging ideas." Then, double-down on listening. Safety starts with people feeling they are being heard and understood. Visit Chapter 8 about listening to learn tips on increasing your skill.

Don't expect changes overnight. Creating an environment where everyone feels comfortable speaking freely will take time, especially when trust is low.

17. How can I speak more concisely?

Here's a simple and powerful approach. The concept is called half-life and it's iteratively refining your core message to its essence. Try this: Find an email message in your draft folder right now. Rewrite it by removing half of the words without losing the core message. Now do it again. Can you condense that message even more?

This works equally well in verbal communication. Pick some content you will be presenting at your next meeting.

Find a quiet place to record yourself speaking. Time it. Play it back and think about how you could cut half the words while still conveying a cohesive, clear message. Record yourself again and aim to make it briefer.

18. What are some tips for asking better questions?

Plan your questions in advance. Wonderfully insightful and illuminating questions don't usually just pop into our minds at the perfect moment.

Often, the more you know about a topic, the more your curiosity is stoked. How many of you, like us, fall into wormholes? Therese went from watching a documentary on Mount Everest to spending hours researching the history of sherpas. If you sense yourself feeling as if you have all the answers, challenge yourself to find the edge of your knowledge. Ask yourself, "What don't I know?"

Frame your questions in a way that gets you more than a passive head nod or yes/no response. Questions that begin with how, where, when, and why require people to think a little deeper and respond with more words. Find more ideas in Chapter 8 about listening.

19. What do I do when there's a language barrier?

Avoid jargon, colloquialisms, and metaphors that could be confusing or misunderstood. Use the simplest language possible.

Mental translations are happening while you're speaking, so make it easier on your listeners by moderating your pace and annunciate clearly. Be observant and watch for signs that people might be confused. Better yet, ask people privately if your pace is working for them and the group.

Your audience may feel self-conscious speaking up in large groups. Don't misinterpret silence to mean they aren't engaged. After posing a question, direct people to discuss it in small groups and encourage them to speak in their native language.

20. I expect pushback on my message. How can I overcome the objections?

When encountering resistance, first understand the objection by listening and staying curious rather than reacting immediately. If a client says, "It's too expensive," instead of replying, "Yes, but we can't control inflation," stay curious to get to what's underlying the objection. Sometimes the root cause of the resistance is different from what you think. Maybe it's not an issue with cost but timing, or the client sees the value but needs help convincing their boss.

Listening well allows you to understand and empathize with the client, so you can partner with them in addressing the roadblock versus being on opposite sides.

In Chapter 9 ("Serve the Purpose"), we explore how any response or reaction is an offer to build upon. Using the improv principle, "Yes, and" allows you to build on the conversation and not block it. It signals acknowledgment and respect and creates a path to new alternatives.

21. What if my values seem to be in conflict with the values of my participants?

Values are complex. We do not all prioritize the same qualities. This is not inherently problematic. In fact, it can be good: Diversity makes us stronger. You do want to feel ethically aligned with your core values, though. Whether or not you share your beliefs explicitly, you can often influence others through behavior that demonstrates what you care about. Understanding and respecting others' values will also help you lead effectively.

In a situation where you feel your values are in direct conflict with those you are engaging with in ways that cause tension or obstructions in the room, you may wish to open an explicit values conversation. Deepening your understanding of what people care about is as important as sharing your own values.

In rare cases, we find we may need to set boundaries or sever relationships. If you feel unable to act in alignment with your values in any relationship, it is worth reflecting on the worth of that connection.

For more about identifying your own values and behaving in alignment with them, start with Chapter 3 ("Model Values and Beliefs"). You may also find tips in Chapter 8 ("Listening") and Chapter 10 ("Balance Risk and Safety").

22. What about interactivity and experiential activities to engage groups?

There is a plethora of experiential activities designed to deepen understanding, build connection and inclusion, and aid retention. We are great fans of interactive approaches. In this book, we did not dive into experiential activities explicitly, but Kat's book, *Training to Imagine,* is a wonderful resource for activities and how to facilitate using them.

What Comes Next?

You may remember that back at the beginning of this book, we used the analogy of cooking. Whether you are looking for down-and-dirty recipes or plan to develop master-chef-level facilitation prowess, we look forward to supporting you in your development.

Check out *thefacilitationadvantage.com* to join our facilitation community and receive ongoing tips, tools, and support.

And, of course, as any good facilitator would, we look forward to hearing from you. Let us know about your successes, challenges, questions, and insights.

Together, we look forward to bringing the Facilitation Advantage to the world!

Acknowledgments

When diving into a new book, we often flip to the acknowledgments first, eager to peek behind the curtain to get a glimpse of the "story behind the story." If you find this book helpful, know that credit for its creation is shared among some wonderful human beings we wish to recognize here.

From Therese

I wish to acknowledge Proteus International, specifically Erika Andersen, founder, and Jeff Mitchell, president. I was introduced to the skills of facilitation through a train-the-trainer experience in a Proteus leadership development program in 2006 and it changed the trajectory of my career. Long before I knew what facilitation skills were, Jeff and Erika were perfecting Proteus's methodology, which defined specific "contributions" in concrete behavioral terms that were easy to understand intellectually but challenging to master in practice. Especially through Jeff's coaching and encouragement, the skills eventually became second nature, and I was leading more effectively in a wide range of contexts — not just a training room. It is with their blessing that this book was written. I am profoundly grateful to Proteus for the permission to use and build on their original content.

To my husband, Mike. My ultimate cheerleader. With you by my side, every triumph is sweeter, every challenge more surmountable, and every moment more special. DITYILYT? To my children, Colin and Grace, you will always be the fire in my heart, the greatest joy in my memories, and the reason writing this book was so important to me. To the many family, friends, colleagues, and clients, who often asked, "How's the book coming along?" – your encouragement has been a gift beyond measure.

From Kat

Just like raising a child, bringing a book to fruition requires a village. Among the very many people who have mentored, supported, and inspired me are the creative and positive members of the Applied Improvisation Network and The Mopco Improv Theatre, the wise and kind folks at the Learning Development Accelerator, my colleagues and thought-partners, John Register and Vladimir Bychkovsky, and my besties in the 11 Minutes to Mars crew.

My Koppett & Company colleagues, Chris Esparza and Livia Walker, have been instrumental in the development of this work, and a joy to play with. My family has always offered support, a high bar, and a reason to aim to be my best self, personally and professionally. I am more than thankful for Lia, Michael, David, Karen, Mom and Dad.

From Us

We would also like to thank the many people who reviewed and offered feedback on early versions of the manuscript, including, Shawn Adams, Erika Andersen, Margaux Arieta-Pelli, Maria Ayoob, Micaela Blei, Jean Bonifas, Sarah Brown, Brenny Campbell, Ted DesMaisons Chris Esparza, Kimberly Hill, Marie Holive, Jeanne Lambin, Erica Marx, Jeff Mitchell, Ryan Rogers, Ada Roseti, Catie Sack, Craig Schaefer, Chris Taylor, Stacy Waltz, and Cathy Windschitl.

Finally we are indebted to the publishing team at BDI, especially Brent Darnell and Casey McConnell, who were the perfect sherpas, guiding us every step of the way to make this book a reality and to Derek Walker, our talented graphis and web designer.

INDEX

About the Authors

Photo credit: Dianne Chappell

Kat Koppett is the president and founder of Koppett & Company. She holds a BFA in drama from New York University and an MA in organizational psychology from Columbia University. She is also a Certified Professional Co-Active Coach, and co-director of the Mopco Improv Theatre.

Her book, *Training to Imagine: Practical Improvisational Theatre Techniques to Enhance Creativity, Teamwork, Leadership, and Learning*, is considered a seminal work in the field of applied improvisation and is used by professionals around the world. In 2019, Kat received NASAGA's Ifill-Raynolds Lifetime Achievement Award for her work in furthering experiential learning. She is a founding member of the Applied Improvisation Network and the host of the podcast "Performance Shift: The Art of Successfully Navigating Change."

koppett.com

Photo credit: Fokus Photography

Therese Miclot operates her own consultancy, Therese Miclot, LLC, and brings two decades of experience in developing individuals into competent and compassionate leaders. With insights drawn from exposure to the most intricate leadership challenges, she is deeply aligned with the landscape of modern business. She has a keen understanding of what is required to drive leadership performance. Known for her deep listening skills, she tailors her approach to her clients' needs and challenges.

Additionally, she serves as the Director of Facilitation Excellence at Proteus International, where she's a driving force in equipping leaders with everyday facilitation skills. Her track record spans tech, manufacturing, banking, media and retail including Meta, New York Stock Exchange, Madison Square Garden, FanDuel, Flutter, Grant Thornton, Citi, BNY Mellon, and Rockwell Automation.

With a master's degree in Industrial/Organizational Psychology, she brings a disciplined approach to leadership development, while finding joy in creating practical and simple solutions to clients' needs.

theresemiclot.com

To get more Facilitation Advantage tips, tools, support and references, go to: thefacilitationadvantage.com

Milton Keynes UK
Ingram Content Group UK Ltd.
UKHW021112200524
442968UK00015B/1075